SHORT CUTS FOR ROUND LAYOUTS

THIRD EDITION

Short Cuts for Round Layouts

THIRD EDITION

Joseph J. Kaberlein

Bruce

A division of Benziger Bruce & Glencoe, Inc.
Beverly Hills

KABERLEIN SHEET METAL SERIES
- **Short Cuts for Round Layouts**
- **Triangulation Short-Cut Layouts**
- **Air Conditioning Metal Layout**

Bruce
A division of Benziger Bruce & Glencoe, Inc.
8701 Wilshire Boulevard
Beverly Hills, California 90211

Library of Congress Catalog Card Number 73–79333

Second printing, 1975

SHORT CUTS FOR ROUND LAYOUTS is intended for use as a text in vocational, trade, and technical high schools and in teacher training schools where pattern layout is being taught. Each problem is practical and adaptable, drawn to scale with dimensions that are of ample size for metal construction. This book has also been designed to serve as a text and guide for men in the sheet metal field.

A special aid for the reader has been incorporated into this book. Each projection line in each diagram is marked by an arrow to show the direction in which the line should be drawn. This feature will enable anyone—students as well as more experienced men—to determine at a glance the means to obtain the various profile developments without studying the text at any great length.

A course in beginning drawing that embraces geometrical construction and isometric views is a prerequisite for understanding and making use of this text. The student with little practical experience in sheet metal layout will find it best to study the first plate in each section before attempting the more complex layouts that follow.

Preface v

PART ONE

PARALLEL LINE DEVELOPMENT

CONTENTS

PART TWO

RADIAL LINE DEVELOPMENT

CONTENTS

PART ONE
Parallel Line Development

PLATE 1   GROOVED LOCK SEAM

This type of seam is used when joining together two or more pieces of metal and when making round or rectangular pipes of metal No. 20 gauge and lighter.

Figure 1 shows how seam allowance is made when two pieces of metal are to be seamed together, using a $^3/_8$-in. grooved lock seam. The allowance to be made on each piece of metal equals $1\,^1/_2$ times the size of seam desired.

This project calls for a $^3/_8$-in. grooved lock seam; therefore, a $^9/_{16}$-in. allowance is made on each piece. A $^3/_8$-in. line is marked on one side of each piece of metal, and that same amount is turned up, one hooked to the inside and one to the outside, as shown in Figure 2.

To assemble the pieces of metal, they are locked together as shown in Figure 3. Then, with the aid of a hand grooving tool, the locks are flattened and the top piece of metal is brought down to form a pocket as in Figure 4. This will prevent the locks from dismembering.

Figure 5 shows a perspective view of two pieces of metal that are grooved lock seamed together.

PLATE 2   HAMMER-GROOVED LOCK SEAM

This type of seam is used for joining long sheets or small pieces of metal and to lock retangular pipes. It is an efficient seam which is easy to form and may be used on No. 20 gauge and lighter metal.

It is assumed that No. 24-gauge metal is used in this project. Figure 1 shows how the patterns are laid out and the seam allowances are made. On Pattern No. 1, a $^3/_8$-in. allowance is made for the single lock. The allowance for the double lock on Pattern No. 2 equals twice the allowance for the single lock plus $^1/_{16}$ in. Therefore, Pattern No. 2 has one $^3/_8$-in. space and one $^7/_{16}$-in. space.

To form the locks on the patterns, turn a $^3/_8$-in. lock on Pattern No. 2, as in Figure 2. Reverse the sheet so that the lock just turned faces down. Now, bend up the double lock to about a 60-deg. angle as in Figure 3. Turn the single lock on Pattern No. 1 to about a 60-deg. angle as in Figure 4. Insert the single lock on Pattern No. 1, in the double lock on Pattern No. 2 as in Figure 5.

To flatten the lock and form a pocket to prevent dismemberment, use a short piece of band iron which has been bent so that it may be firmly held with the left hand. Place this piece of band iron behind the double lock as shown in Figure 6. Keep the band next to the seam, and use a mallet to strike the lock seam and the band with each blow. This flattens the lock seam, and the band iron offsets the metal and forms a pocket as in Figure 7, preventing the lock from coming apart.

PLATE 1

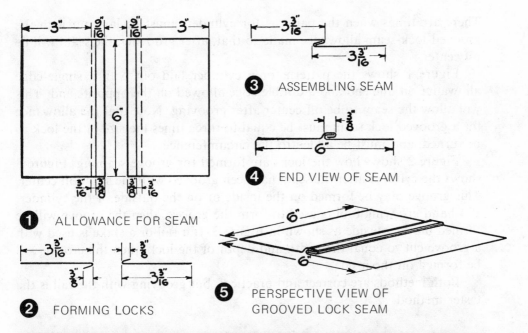

1 ALLOWANCE FOR SEAM

2 FORMING LOCKS

3 ASSEMBLING SEAM

4 END VIEW OF SEAM

5 PERSPECTIVE VIEW OF GROOVED LOCK SEAM

PLATE 2

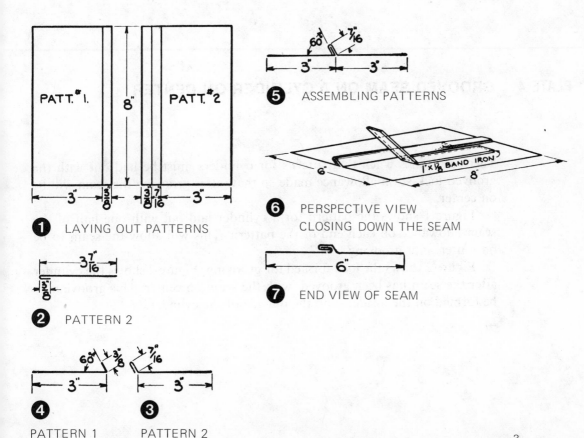

1 LAYING OUT PATTERNS

2 PATTERN 2

4 PATTERN 1

3 PATTERN 2

5 ASSEMBLING PATTERNS

6 PERSPECTIVE VIEW CLOSING DOWN THE SEAM

7 END VIEW OF SEAM

PLATE 3   GROOVED SEAM ON A CYLINDER OFF CENTER

There are times when the patterns for cylinders must be laid out with the grooved-lock-seam allowance made so that, after grooving, the seam will be off center.

Figure 1 shows the pattern for a cylinder laid out with a single-edge allowance on one end and a double edge allowed on the opposite end. This will allow the seam to be off center after grooving. Note that the allowance for a grooved lock seam must be equal to three times the size of the lock to be turned, and must be added to the circumference.

Figure 2 shows how the locks are formed for groove seaming. Figure 3 shows the cylinder after the seam has been grooved with the seam off center. This groove may be formed on the inside or on the outside of the cylinder. If a hand grooving tool is used to form the groove, then the groove will be formed on the outside as shown in Figure 3. If a rail or a stake is used with a groove cut to equal the width and depth of the lock, then the groove will be formed on the inside.

Both methods are correct and practical, but grooving with the rail is the faster method.

PLATE 4   GROOVED SEAM ON A CYLINDER ON CENTER

There are times when the patterns for cylinders must be laid out with the grooved-lock-seam allowance made so that, after grooving the seam will be on center.

Figure 1 shows the pattern for a cylinder laid out with one half of the seam allowance on each end of the pattern. This will allow the seam to be on center after grooving.

Figure 2 shows the lock formed for grooving. Figure 3 shows the cylinder after the seam has been grooved, with the seam on center. This groove may be formed on the inside or on the outside of the cylinder.

PLATE 3

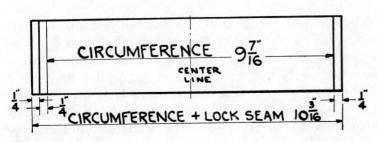

1 PIPE PATTERN

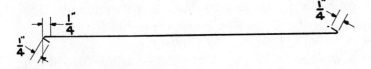

2 LOCK SEAM BENT

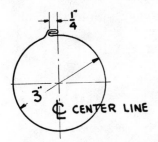

3 GROOVED LOCK SEAM
OFF CENTER

PLATE 4

2 LOCK SEAM FORMED

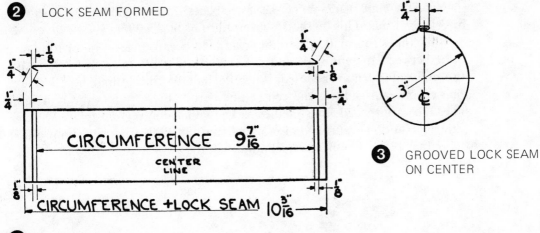

3 GROOVED LOCK SEAM
ON CENTER

1 PIPE PATTERN

PLATE 5   RIVETED LAP SEAM

When seaming metals of No. 18 gauge and heavier, the riveting lap seam is used. While No. 18-gauge metal may be groove seamed, it is not recommended unless a special grade of metal is used or there is a definite reason why a grooved seam should be used.

Metals lighter than No. 18 gauge also may be riveted, because there are cases where it is absolutely necessary that riveting be used. The amount of lap to be allowed and the distance the holes are to be spaced apart will vary in accordance with the gauge of metal that is used.

The table on page 9 shows the lap allowance, the rivet spacing, and the size rivets that are to be used for the different gauges of metal:

Gauge	Lap Allowance in In.	Rivet Space in In.	Size Rivets	
28	$1/4$	$2 1/2$	12	oz.
26	$1/4$	$2 1/2$	1	lb.
24	$3/8$	$2 1/2$	$1 1/2$	lb.
22	$3/8$	3	$1 1/2$	lb.
20	$3/8$	3	$2 1/2$	lb.
18	$1/2$	3	3	lb.
16	$1/2$	$3 1/2$	4	lb.
14	$1/2$	$3 1/2$	5	lb.
12	$5/8$	4	8	lb.
10	$3/4$	4	10	lb.

Figure 1 is dimensioned only to illustrate the method used in laying out a riveting lap seam. It is assumed that No. 18-gauge metal is used in this project. To lay out a riveting lap seam as in Figure 1, draw a $1/2$-in. line on either side of the piece of metal. On this line the hole spaces are laid out. If possible, they should be laid out from the center line of the sheet as shown in Figure 1.

Find the center and mark the hole spaces on each side of it, as shown, by 3-in. spacings. This method is referred to as *making the holes from center*.

Sometimes this method cannot be applied because there will be too much space between the end hole and the end of the sheet of iron. In that case, another method may be used, whereby half of the desired hole space is marked on each side of the center line. From these points the remaining holes then are spaced. This method is known as *marking the holes off center*. Either method is accurate and practical and makes the pattern foolproof so that either piece may be reversed and the holes will match at all times.

PLATE 5

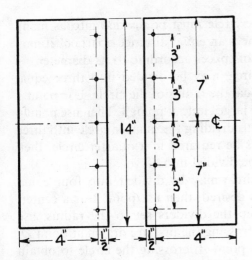

1 METHOD OF LAYING OUT HOLES

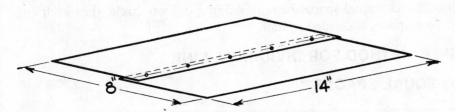

2 PERSPECTIVE VIEW OF RIVETED LAP SEAM

3 END VIEW OF RIVETED SEAM

PLATE 6 DIVIDING QUARTER CIRCLES

When making cylindrical objects, the circle must be divided into as many spaces as may be desired, with all spaces an equal distance apart; or it may be divided into the required number of spaces according to its diameter.

Figure 1 shows how a quarter circle may be divided into three equal spaces, by spanning the dividers to equal the radius of the circle. Use point 1 as a center to strike an arc crossing the large circle at point 3. Then use point 4 as a center, strike an arc at point 2, thus dividing the quarter circle into three equal spaces. Should six equal spaces be required in a quarter circle, then each one of the three spaces should be divided in half.

Figure 2 shows how a quarter circle may be divided into four equal spaces. Set the dividers to any radius desired, then use point 1 as a center, striking an arc toward point D. Keep the dividers set to the radius, use point 5 as a center, and strike an arc crossing the first arc drawn at point D. Draw a straight line from point D to point A, crossing the circle to obtain point 3. Again set the dividers to any radius desired. Draw arcs from points 1 and 3, 3 and 5, to cross each other at points E and F. Draw straight lines from points E and F toward point A, obtaining points 2 and 4 which will divide the circle into four equal spaces.

Should eight equal spaces be required in a quarter circle, then each one of the four spaces is divided in half.

PLATE 7   SIMPLE METHOD FOR DIVIDING A LINE
INTO EQUAL SPACES

Line A to B may be any length desired. Line A to C may be any length that will represent a number of equal spaces that are divided by even inches on the ruler.

Example: Line A to B is equal to $54\frac{7}{16}$ in. and should be divided into nine equal spaces. Then 7 is the nearest number that will allow nine equal spaces on the ruler without encountering fractions. Thus, $7 \times 9 = 63$, with one end of the ruler set on point A. The other end of the ruler then is moved up or down until number 63 on the ruler crosses line B–C at point C. Now, with the aid of a pencil or scratch awl, place a mark from A to C at every 7 in. such as from 7 to 56 in., as shown. Draw a straight line down from each division point on line A–C to intersect line A–B. This will give the required number of equal spaces on line A–B without the use of the dividers. This method of dividing a line is fast and accurate.

PLATE 6

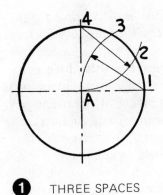

1 THREE SPACES

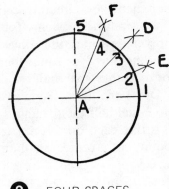

2 FOUR SPACES

PLATE 7

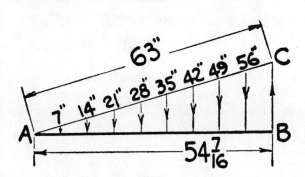

PLATE 8   DIVIDING INTO FOUR, EIGHT, OR SIXTEEN EQUAL SPACES

Linear measurements or circumferences are divided into four, eight, or sixteen, and six, twelve, or twenty-four equal spaces to represent rivet or bolt holes for joining to another object.

To divide a line into four equal spaces as in Figure 1, set the dividers by trial and error until they span half the distance 1 to 5. Then use points 1 and 5 as centers. Draw arcs to strike each other on a tangent at point 3. Span the dividers to equal half the distance 1 to 3. Use points 1 and 3 as centers. Draw arcs to strike each other on a tangent at point 2. Keep the dividers set and use point 3 as a center, striking an arc at point 4. The result will be four equal spaces.

To divide a line into eight equal spaces as in Figure 2, span the dividers to equal half the distance 1 to 9. Use points 1 and 9 as centers. Draw arcs to strike each other on a tangent at point 5. Span the dividers to equal half the distance 1 to 5. Use points 1 and 5 as centers to draw arcs striking each other on a tangent at point 3. Keep the dividers set, and using 5 as a center, strike an arc at point 7. Span the dividers to equal half the distance 3 to 5. Draw arcs from 3 and 5 to strike on a tangent at point 4. Keep the dividers set, and strike arcs at points 2, 6, and 8 from point 7.

To divide a line into sixteen equal spaces as in Figure 3, use the above procedure to obtain the division points. Use points 1 and 17 as centers to strike arcs on a tangent at point 9. Use 1 and 9 as centers to strike on a tangent at point 5. Keep the dividers set to strike an arc at 13. Use 5 and 9 as centers to strike on a tangent at point 7. Keep the dividers set to strike an arc at 11 and 3; also use point 13 as a center to strike an arc at point 15. Use 9 and 7 as centers to strike on a tangent at point 8. Keep the dividers set to strike an arc at 6; also use point 3 as a center to strike arcs at 4 and 2. Use points 11 and 15 as centers to strike arcs at 10 and 12, 14 and 16.

PLATE 8

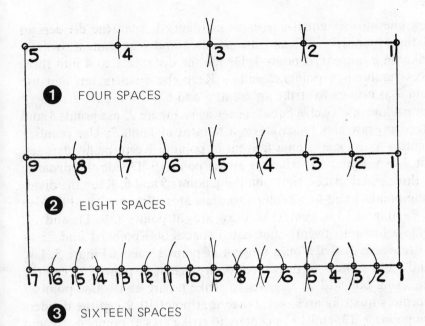

1 FOUR SPACES

2 EIGHT SPACES

3 SIXTEEN SPACES

PLATE 9 **DIVIDING INTO SIX, TWELVE,**

OR TWENTY-FOUR EQUAL SPACES

To divide a line into six equal spaces as in Figure 1, span the dividers to equal half the distance 1 to 7, and use points 1 and 7 as centers to draw arcs to strike on a tangent at point 4. Divide the distance 1 to 4 into three equal spaces resulting in points 2 and 3. Keep the dividers set, and use points 4 and 7 as centers to strike an arc at 5 and 6.

To divide a line into twelve equal spaces as in Figure 2, use points 1 and 13 as centers to draw arcs to strike on a tangent at point 7. Use points 1 and 7 as centers to draw arcs on a tangent at point 4. Keep the dividers set, using point 7 as a center to strike an arc at point 10. Divide the distance 4 to 7 into three equal spaces, thus obtaining points 5 and 6. Keep the dividers set, using points 1 and 4 as centers, to draw arcs at points 2 and 3. Also use points 7, 10, and 13 as centers to draw arcs at points 8, 9, 11, and 12.

To divide a line into twenty-four equal spaces, use points 1 and 25 as centers to draw arcs to strike on a tangent at point 13, as in Figure 3. Use points 1 and 13 as centers to draw arcs on a tangent at point 7. Keep the dividers set, using point 13 as a center to strike an arc at 19. Use points 7 and 13 as centers to strike arcs on a tangent at point 10. Keep the dividers set, and use points 7, 13, and 19 as centers to strike arcs at points 4, 16, and 22. Divide the distance 10 to 13 into three equal spaces.

Keep the dividers set, and use points 10, 7, 4, and 1 as centers to strike arcs at points 9, 8, 6, 5, 3, and 2. Also use points 13, 16, 19, 22, and 25 as centers to strike arcs at points 14, 15, 17, 18, 20, 22, and 23.

PLATE 10   **LARGE AND SMALL CYLINDERS**

When placing a small cylinder centered inside a larger cylinder so that the holes on the smaller cylinder will align with the holes on the larger cylinder as shown in Figure 1, the holes for each must be laid out on the flat, so that each pattern will have the same number of holes spaced equally apart as in Figures 2 and 3.

The holes may be laid out by using the same method as in the previous plate, dividing a line into twelve equal spaces.

PLATE 9

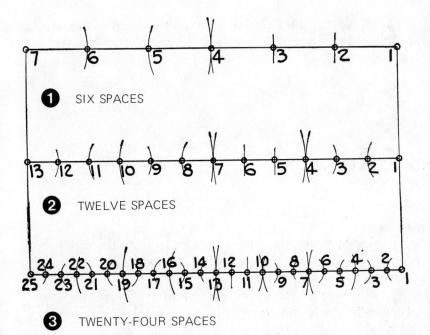

1 SIX SPACES

2 TWELVE SPACES

3 TWENTY-FOUR SPACES

PLATE 10

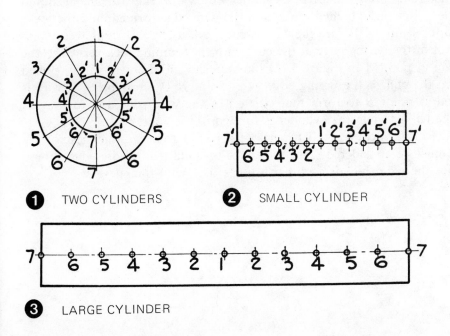

1 TWO CYLINDERS

2 SMALL CYLINDER

3 LARGE CYLINDER

PLATE 11   PLACING HOLES ON ANGLE IRON

When spacing holes on angle iron, the holes should be placed on half the distance of *A*, or to the center line of the inside of the web as shown in Plate 11.

PLATE 12   FORMING WIRE EDGE

To reinforce an edge by enclosing wire or rod with metal, the metal to be allowed is equal to $2\frac{1}{2}$ times the thickness of the wire or rod to be enclosed as shown in Figure 2.

To form the wire-edge allowance by the use of the brake, two bends must be made. The first bend should be equal to the minimum amount that the brake will bend (about $\frac{3}{32}$ in. as in Fig. 3) and be bent up at about a 45-deg. angle.

The second bend will be the remainder of the allowance and should be bent up to less than 90 deg. on the outside bend or equal to about 97 deg. on the inside, as shown in Figure 4.

With the aid of a mallet, the metal may be bent over the wire, and the front edge may be dressed up, if necessary, with a square-faced hammer, enclosing the wire as in Figure 1.

When reinforcing the top of a cylinder with a wire edge, the metal should be rolled, then straightened out again, the wire edge formed, and the locks turned for seaming. Before the wire is enclosed, it should be allowed to extend out of the wiring edge at the end, with the seaming lock turned to the inside as at point *A* in Figure 5. At the opposite end the wire will be pulled in from the end of the wiring edge as at point *B*. A short piece of wire is inserted at point *B* to form that portion of the wire edge and to prevent from flattening when the cylinder is formed in the rolls.

When using heavy metal to enclose a round rod, the thickness of the metal must be considered. The allowance of metal for a wire edge should be twice the wire thickness plus five times the metal thickness.

PLATE 11

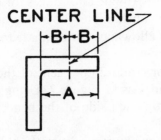

CENTER LINE

B B

A

PLATE 12

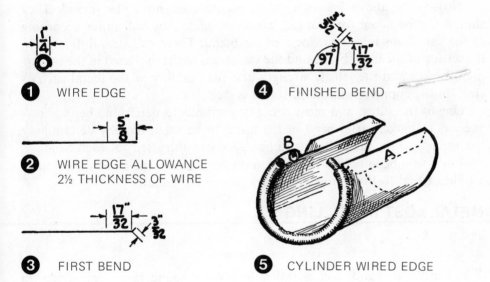

① WIRE EDGE

② WIRE EDGE ALLOWANCE
2½ THICKNESS OF WIRE

③ FIRST BEND

④ FINISHED BEND

⑤ CYLINDER WIRED EDGE

PLATE 13   BEND ALLOWANCE

This plate shows the approximate allowances for bends on inside dimensions as in Figure 1, and the subtractions for bends on outside dimensions as in Figure 3.   The metal allowances to be made for each bend depend on the thickness of metal.

For inside dimensions, add 20 per cent of the thickness of the metal on each side of the bend lines as in Figure 2. Using .25-in. metal thickness, the allowance to be made on each side of the bend lines in Figure 2 would be .25 × .20 = .05.

For outside dimensions 80 per cent of the thickness of the metal should be subtracted on each side of the bend lines as in Figure 4. Using .25-in. metal thickness, the metal to be subtracted from each side of the bend lines in Figure 4 would be .25 × 80 = .20.

NOTE: The above figures may be accurate on hot-rolled metal. They should not be taken for granted, however, since they will differ according to the variations in the hardness of the metal. There will be a difference in the setting of the hand brake and the variations in the dies used in the power-press brakes and the tensile strength and the ductility of the metal such as steel, brass, copper, aluminum, stainless steel, etc.

One of the surest and most accurate methods to determine bend allowances is to make a trial bend of the metal to be used, thereby determining the amount of the metal that is to be added or subtracted for each bend.

For a safe bend on aluminum and on some brass, the bend should have a radius equal to three times the thickness of the metal.

PLATE 14   METAL LOST IN ROLLING

When metal or band iron is rolled to form a round hoop or cylinder, a shrinkage takes place in the course of rolling. This reduces the inside diameter equal to one thickness of the metal, but increases the outside diameter equal to one thickness of the metal.

This plate shows the different diameters that may be obtained when no allowance or reduction is made in the circumference (to compensate for the thickness of the metal) before the pattern is rolled into a cylinder or hoop.

When no allowance or reduction has been made in the circumference in accordance to the thickness of the metal, after the pattern has been rolled into a cylinder, the diameter to which the circumference was figured will appear as the mean diameter. The inside diameter will be reduced equal to one thickness of the metal, and outside the diameter will be increased equal to one thickness of the metal as shown. Here $\frac{1}{4}$-in. metal has been rolled to a 20-inch diameter cylinder.

When the inside diameter is desired, add to the given diameter one thickness of the metal. In this project $20 + \frac{1}{4} = 20\frac{1}{4}$ in.; thus the circumference will be $20.25 \times 3.1416 = 63.61$ in. When the outside diameter is desired, subtract from the given diameter one thickness of the metal. In this project 20 minus $\frac{1}{4}$ equals $19\frac{3}{4}$ in., and the circumference will be $19.75 \times 3.1416 = 62.05$ in.

PLATE 13

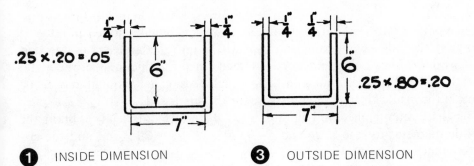

.25 × .20 = .05

.25 × .80 = .20

1 INSIDE DIMENSION

3 OUTSIDE DIMENSION

2 STRETCH OUT

4 STRETCH OUT

PLATE 14

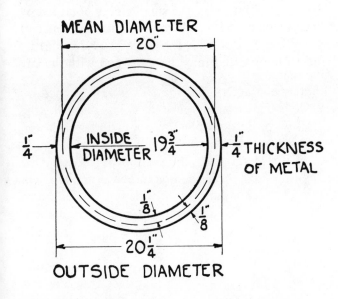

MEAN DIAMETER 20"

INSIDE DIAMETER 19¾"

¼ THICKNESS OF METAL

⅛" ⅛"

OUTSIDE DIAMETER 20¼"

PLATE 15   SMALL AND LARGE ENDS

When patterns are laid out for round stacks, a small and a large end must be made so that the small end of one joint will fit into the large end of another.

Section 1 shows the diameters obtained when the thickness of the metal is added to the given diameter before calculating the circumference. To obtain the inside given diameter A–A, for the small end, $20 + \frac{1}{4} = 20\frac{1}{4}$ in.; thus the circumference will be $20.25 \times 3.1416 = 63.61$ in. To obtain the inside diameter for the large end B–B, $20\frac{1}{2} + \frac{1}{4} = 20\frac{3}{4}$ in., and the circumference will be 65.18 in.

The above method is true and accurate, but it will not allow the small end to enter the large end to make a riveting connection.

When the small end must enter into the large end far enough to make a riveting seam connection, and if the inside diameter of the small end must be maintained, then an extra allowance must be added to the circumference of the inside diameter of the large end to facilitate connection. The inside diameter of the small end is 20 in.; then $20 + \frac{1}{4} = 20\frac{1}{4}$ in., and the circumference will be 63.61 in. The circumference for the inside diameter of the large end will be equal to the circumference for the small end plus seven times the thickness of the metal. In this case $7 \times \frac{1}{4} = 1\frac{3}{4}$ or $1.75 + 63.61 = 65.36$ in. This allows the seam to be loose enough to make an easy connection.

If a looser connection is desired, then eight or nine times the thickness of the metal may be added.

Section 2 shows the diameter of the large end C–C and the mean diameter D–D when the thickness of the metal is not added to the given diameter.

When the inside diameter of the small end does not have to be maintained, then the circumference for the large end is obtained, which will be $20 \times 3.1416 = 62.83$ in. The circumference for the small end is obtained by subtracting seven times the thickness of the metal from the circumference of the large end. In this case $7 \times \frac{1}{4} = 1\frac{3}{4}$ or 1.75, then $62.83 - 1.75 = 61.08$ in. This allows the small end to be inserted into the large end without any difficulty.

PLATE 15

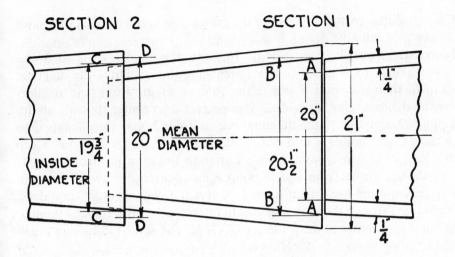

PLATE 16   ELLIPSE DRAWN BY COMPASS

To draw an ellipse to any dimension, the center lines referred to as the major and minor axis must be drawn first.

To construct an ellipse as in Plate 16, draw the major axis *A* to *B* and the minor axis *C* to *D* equal to the dimensions shown. Draw the diagonal line *D* to *B*; then use point *B* as a center to draw an arc from point 1 intersecting the diagonal line at point 2. Use point 1 as a center to draw an arc from point *D* intersecting the diagonal line at point 3. Use the distance 2 to 3 as a radius, and points *A* and *B* as centers to draw arcs at *E* and *F*. Keep the dividers set and use point *E* as a center to draw an arc from *A* to *G* crossing the arc drawn from *E*. Use point *F* as a center to draw an arc from *B* to *H* crossing the arc drawn from *F*. Bisect the distance *D*–*G* and draw a straight line through the bisecting arcs to intersect the center line at point *J*. Use point *J* as a center to draw the arc *G*, *D*, *H*. The same radius length will be used to draw the arc *G*, *C*, *H*.

PLATE 17   ELLIPSE DRAWN BY USE OF STRING

To draw an ellipse by use of string to construct the curves, draw the major axis *A* to *B*, and the minor axis *C* to *D*, equal to the dimensions shown. Use one half of the major axis as a radius; then use point *C* as a center to draw an arc at *E* and *F*. Stick a sharp pin in points *E* and *F*, fasten a piece of string or fine wire to the pins, the length to equal the distance *E*–*C*–*F*. This string should be long enough, when pulled tight, to allow the center of the pencil point to rest on the center of point *C*. Swing the pencil (inside of the string), drawing an arc from *C* to *A* and *C* to *B*. Repeat the procedure to draw the arc from *D* to *A* and *D* to *B* completing the ellipse.

PLATE 16

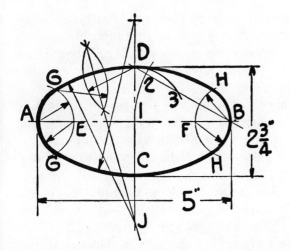

PLATE 17

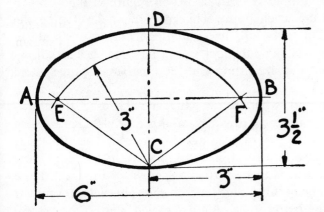

PLATE 18   ROUND TWO-PIECE 45-DEG. ANGLE

For a side profile as in Figure 1, draw a curved heel and throat to a 45-deg. angle. Then bisect the heel curve, and draw a straight line of indefinite length from the center point *R* through the division point on the heel curve. Draw a line squaring from the base line *A–B* at point *B* to intersect the slant line drawn from the radius point *R* at point *C*.

Due to the difficulty in forming the peening lock at the throat as deep as at the back, the thickness of the metal used is taken off the side profile at the throat from the slant line *C–R* to point *D*. Draw a line from point *C* to *D* to obtain the new miter line. This will allow the angle to finish at 45 deg. when assembled.

Draw a half circle below the side profile; divide it into equal spaces and number each as shown. Project straight lines from each point on the half circle to intersect the slant miter line *C–D* as shown in Figure 1.

To lay out Pattern No. 1 as in Figure 2, stretch the circumference on a straight line as *A–B*. Then divide it into twice the number of spaces shown in the half circle in Figure 1, and number each point as shown in Figure 2. To obtain the height for Pattern No. 1, take the heights from line *A–B* to the slant line *C–D*, beginning at point 5 in Figure 1, and transfer these heights to their respective numbered vertical lines in Figure 2; then draw a freehand curved line through each point. This method of developing the pattern will allow the seam to be on the side after forming the pattern. Allow a double edge for a peening edge lock on Pattern No. 1. This allowance will vary according to the size fitting and the number of gauge metal used.

When large fittings are made where heavy-gauge metal is used, the allowance for the double edge may be $\frac{3}{8}$ to $\frac{1}{2}$ in., and the single edge may be $\frac{3}{16}$ to $\frac{1}{4}$ in., depending on the size of peening edge desired. The allowance of metal at each end of the pattern for a grooved lock seam shall equal one and one half the size lock that is to be turned as shown in Figure 2. Note the method of notching at the peening edge on each end. This will prevent the edge from opening after the pattern has been assembled. Pattern No. 2 is a duplicate of Pattern No. 1 with only a single-edge allowance. It may be cut from the metal that remains after Pattern No. 1 has been cut.

Form the locks for a grooved lock seam on each pattern as shown in Figure 3. The double for a peening edge lock is formed in the thick-edge turning machine as shown in Figure 4. The single edge is flanged out straight with a turning machine.

Figure 5 shows an assembled angle with the peening edge locks closed.

PLATE 18

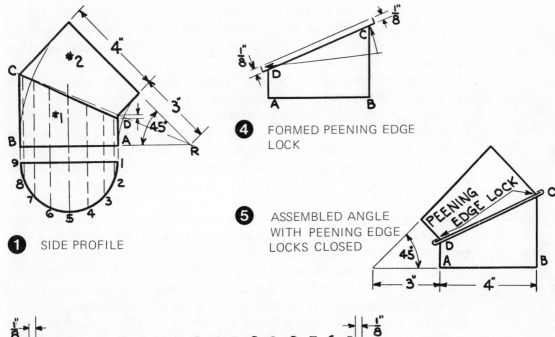

1 SIDE PROFILE

4 FORMED PEENING EDGE LOCK

5 ASSEMBLED ANGLE WITH PEENING EDGE LOCKS CLOSED

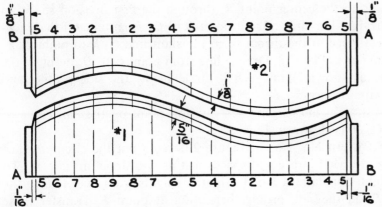

2 DEVELOPED PATTERNS WITH PEENING EDGES

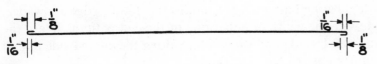

3 FORMING THE LOCK SEAM

PLATE 19   THREE-PIECE ROUND 90-DEG. ELBOW

When drawing a side profile to lay out a round elbow with three or more pieces, the centerpieces or patterns will at all times be twice the width of either one of the endpieces or patterns, regardless of the number of pieces required.

In this problem the center Pattern No. 2 will be twice the width of either one of the end Patterns Nos. 1 and 3.

This is obtained by dividing the heel curve into equal spaces, in order to determine the exact number of equal spaces that the heel curve is to be divided. A simple standard mathematical rule is: The number of pieces required for an elbow times two, then minus two, and the remainder will be the number of equal spaces that the heel curve will be divided. In this problem a 3-piece elbow is required ($3 \times 2 = 6$, $6 - 2 = 4$). The heel curve then is divided into 4 equal spaces as shown in Figure 1. Each endpiece requires one space. The centerpiece requires 2 spaces. This makes the centerpiece twice the width of either one of the endpieces.

For the side profile shown in Figure 1, draw a curved line at the throat and heel at points A and B. Then divide the heel curve into the required number of equal spaces as determined by the mathematical formula. Draw a straight line from the center point R, through the first division space, to intersect the straight line drawn from point B to C. Then take off the thickness of the metal used at the throat from the slant line $C–R$ to point D, in the same manner as in Plate 18. Draw a line from point C to D to obtain the new miter line as shown. Draw a half circle below the side profile, and divide it into equal spaces.

Then draw straight lines from each division point on the half circle to intersect line $C–D$ as shown in Figure 1.

To lay out Pattern No. 1 as in Figure 2, stretch out the circumference on line $A–B$ and divide into equal spaces just as was done in Plate 18. To obtain the heights for Pattern No. 1 take the heights from line $A–B$ to the slant line $C–D$ on the side profile, beginning at point 5. Transfer these heights to the vertical lines on Pattern No. 1; then draw a freehand curved line through each point. Allow a double edge for a peening lock and a grooved lock seam at each end, as shown, in the same manner as in Plate 18. This is the only pattern that needs to be laid out. Pattern No. 3 is identical to Pattern No. 1 with a single-edge allowance for a peening lock. It, therefore, is produced by duplicating Pattern No. 1, minus the double-edge allowance. Pattern No. 2 is twice the width of either one of the end patterns. Place the two end patterns side by side and draw a line along the curved side and at each end to complete Pattern No. 2 as shown.

Form the locks for a grooved lock seam on each piece as shown in Figure 3. Form the peening edges on each piece the same as in the previous plate, and assemble the pieces as shown in Figure 4, so that the seams are on opposite sides.

PLATE 19

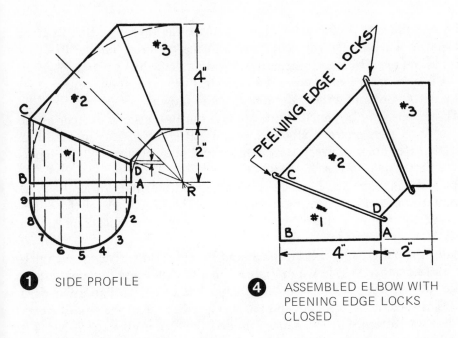

1 SIDE PROFILE

4 ASSEMBLED ELBOW WITH PEENING EDGE LOCKS CLOSED

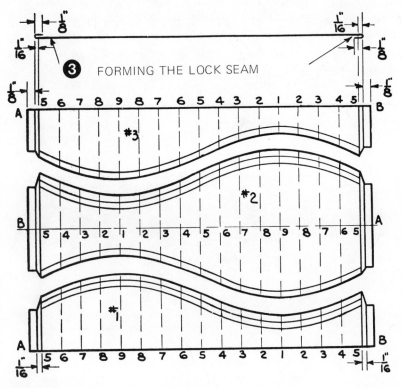

3 FORMING THE LOCK SEAM

2 DEVELOPED PATTERNS WITH PEENING EDGES

25

PLATE 20   ROUND FOUR-PIECE 90-DEG. RIVETED ELBOW

To lay out the side profile as in Figure 1, draw the throat and heel curves at *A* and *B*. Then divide the heel curve into the required number of equal spaces as obtained by the mathematical formula described in Plate 19. Then draw a line from the center point *R* to intersect the vertical line drawn from *B* at point *C*, obtaining the miter line *C–D* as shown.

The patterns for a riveted elbow are laid out in the same manner as the pattern for a peening edge elbow. Lay out Pattern No. 1 as in Figure 2. Mark the rivet holes at every second space and allow a riveting edge lap as shown. Pattern No. 4 is a duplicate of Pattern No. 1.

To make Pattern No. 2, which is twice the width of Pattern No. 1, draw the center line *A–B*; then transfer Pattern No. 1 to each side of the center line *A–B*, completing Pattern No. 2. Pattern No. 3 is a duplicate of Pattern No. 2.

After the patterns have been rolled and the side seams riveted, each pattern must be flanged as shown in Figure 3 to allow the end of one pattern to fit into the end of another when assembling. The throat on Patterns Nos. 2 and 3 is flanged out at one end, and the heel is flanged in at the opposite end. The heel on Pattern No. 1 is flanged in, and the throat on Pattern No. 4 is flanged out as shown in Figure 3.

To assemble the patterns as in Figure 4, begin at the large end with Pattern No. 1, and finish at the small end with Pattern No. 4. This will allow the rivets to rest firmly on the iron rail or stake while riveting. (Note how each pattern is flanged in Figure 4.)

PLATE 20

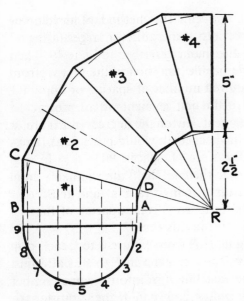

① SIDE PROFILE

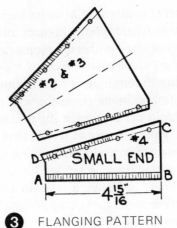

SMALL END

$4\frac{15}{16}$"

③ FLANGING PATTERN

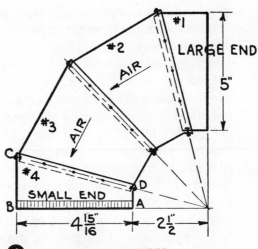

AIR

AIR

LARGE END

5"

SMALL END

$4\frac{15}{16}$" $2\frac{1}{2}$"

④ ASSEMBLED-RIVETED
4 PIECE ELBOW

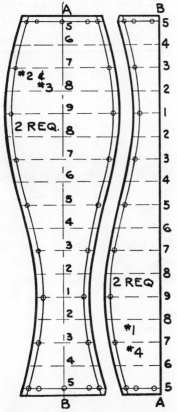

2 REQ.

2 REQ

② DEVELOPED PATTERNS
FOR RIVETING SEAMS

27

PLATE 21   QUARTER PATTERN FOR ROUND ELBOWS

The quarter pattern is a convenient and efficient method of developing patterns for round elbows, angles, or offsets—especially for larger fittings—regardless of the number of pieces or the diameter.

As in previous plates, draw the side profile, and obtain the first segment by dividing the heel curve into the required number of spaces; or apply the shorter method by marking the angle of the first segment with a protractor.

To obtain the degrees in the first segment, divide the degrees in the elbow or angle by the number of spaces that the heel curve would be divided. Thus, in a 4-piece 90-deg. elbow, $4 \times 2 = 8$, $8 - 2 = 6$ spaces, $90 \div 6 = 15$ deg. In Figure 1, draw the center line C–D, then set half the diameter from point R to A, and draw a straight line up crossing the slant line at B.

Referring to Figure 2, draw line F–E to equal one quarter of the circumference or half the diameter times 1.57; in this case, $2.5 \times 1.57 = 3.925$ or about $3^{15}\!/_{16}$. Then transfer the height A–B from Figure 1 to line F–5 in Figure 2. Draw the quarter circle using F as a center and F to 5 as a radius. Divide this quarter circle 1 to 5 and the base line F–E into the same number of spaces. Draw straight lines through points 2, 3, and 4; then transfer the heights 2, 3, and 4 from the end curve to lines 2, 3, and 4 on line F–E. Draw a freehand curve crossing points 1 to 5, and notch the pattern as in Figure 3. Use $\frac{3}{8}$-in. allowance at the bottom and one end as a guide in developing the full pattern.

To develop the full pattern (Figure 4), draw the base line C to equal the full circumference. Transfer the height C–D from Figure 1 to obtain C–D in Figure 4. Divide the base line C into four equal spaces, representing four quarters. Draw straight lines up, crossing line D. Place the quarter pattern with line E–F resting on line D. Beginning at point D–1, draw the curve up from $1E$ to 5. Turn the quarter pattern over end for end, and draw the curve down from 5 to $1E$. Repeat, but with the curved edge of the quarter pattern facing down toward the base line C. Draw the curved line down from 1 to 5, turn the pattern end for end and draw the curved line up from 5 to 1. This completes the pattern except for the allowances for seaming and assembling. If a peening edge is required, draw a parallel line a suitable height above line D and repeat as before with the line E–F resting on the new line.

If riveting is preferred and more than four rivets are required, divide the base line C to equal the number of rivets required, and draw straight lines up crossing the curve at points 1, 2, 3, and 4. Use the same procedure to draw the riveting-edge allowance as for peening.

NOTE: Transfer the height of the heel line and the height of the throat line in side profile, Figure 1, to line F–5 on the heel and line F–5 on the throat in Figure 4 to prevent any variance of those two heights during the development and transferring of the quarter pattern.

PLATE 21

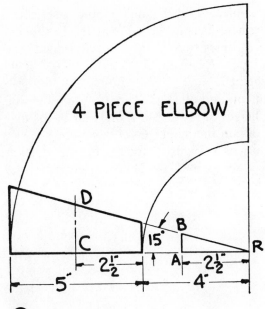

1 SIDE PROFILE

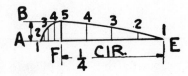

2 1/4 PATTERN

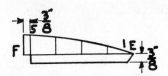

3 NOTCHED PATTERN

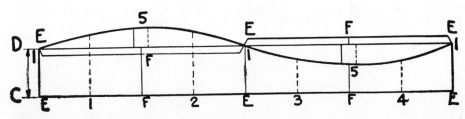

4 FULL PATTERN

29

PLATE 22   THREE-PIECE 45-DEG. ANGLE

To lay out the patterns for a three-piece 45-deg. angle elbow, obtain the degrees for the angle of the first segments, using the same method as for an elbow. That is, the number of pieces times two, minus two, and divide the degrees of the angle by the remainder. *Example*: $3 \times 2 = 6$, $6 - 2 = 4$; $45 \div 4 = 11.25$ deg. of the first segment.

Draw the angle of the first segment, and mark the throat radius and one half of the diameter to obtain the height of A–B. Mark one half of the diameter from the radius point O to obtain the height C–D in Figure 1.

To lay out the one-quarter pattern as in Figure 2 and the full-size pattern as in Figure 3, use the same procedure as in Plate 21 which describes the method for a 90-deg. elbow.

PLATE 23   WELDING ELBOW GORE SEAMS, METAL 18 GAUGE AND LIGHTER

This plate illustrates a practical procedure for preparing the edges of gore sections of round or oval shaped elbows when seams are welded to allow overlapping of metal with a smooth surface and greater strength at the seams.

When gore patterns are layed out, allow $\frac{1}{8}$ inch at each edge of center and end gore; also allow $\frac{1}{8}$ inch at each end of gores for center seam. Place a prick mark on the edge of each seam at each one quarter circumference to facilitate aligning gores. Use the burring machine and set gauge back $\frac{5}{16}$ inch to offset one end of each gore about the depth of bottom roll on machine; roll gores and weld center seams. Next, use the burring machine with the gauge set back $\frac{5}{16}$ inch to shrink or offset small end gore and one edge of center gores to about depth of bottom roll, then also flange out edge of each gore at throat.

This will allow the shrunken end to slide into the flanged end and facilitate assembling and aligning of gore sections to the required angle.

PLATE 22

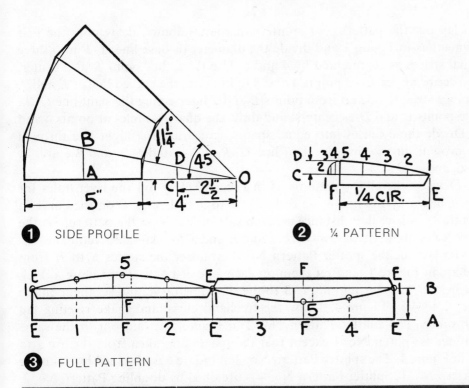

1 SIDE PROFILE

2 ¼ PATTERN

3 FULL PATTERN

PLATE 23

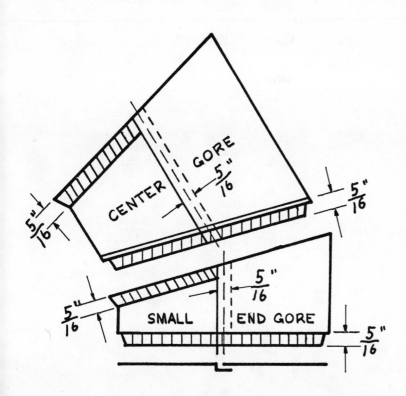

PLATE 24   ROUND ELBOW WITH SPLITTER VANES

To lay out the patterns for splitters in round elbows, draw only the first segment as in Figure 1 and divide the diameter or base line $A-B$ into three equal spaces as represented by 4 and 8. Use the radius point R as a center, and scribe an arc from points 4 and 8 to intersect the curved line at E and J. Draw a straight line up from points E and J intersecting the slant line $O-R$. Use points C and D as centers, and draw the quarter circles at points 4 and 8. Divide these circles into equal spaces, and draw a straight line through each point intersecting the slant line $O-R$ at 2–3 and 6–7, and the arcs at $F-G$ and $K-L$.

Develop the elbow patterns as in Figure 3. Lay out the rivet holes for the splitters by obtaining the distance N to J and N to E on the curve in Figure 1, and set that distance on each side of line N on the pattern. Set the rivet holes about $\frac{1}{4}$ in. away from line E and J to facilitate riveting.

To lay out the splitter Pattern No. 1, transfer the spaces E to H from the arc in Figure 1, and set them on each side of point H in Figure 4. Pick the heights 1 to 4 from line $A-B$ to the slant line $O-R$, and set them on the lines 1 to 4 in Figure 4. Draw the freehand curve and make riveting lap allowance. The splitter Pattern No. 2 in Figure 5 is laid out in the same manner as splitter No. 1 except that the spaces are taken from the arc J to M in Figure 1. The splitter Pattern No. 3 in Figure 6 is obtained by doubling Pattern No. 1. Splitter Pattern No. 4 is obtained by doubling Pattern No. 2.

The front view in Figure 2 shows how the riveting laps are turned and the splitters riveted in place.

PLATE 24

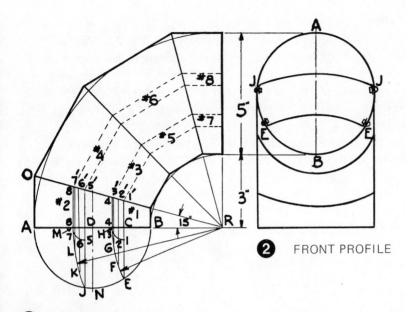

2 FRONT PROFILE

1 SIDE PROFILE

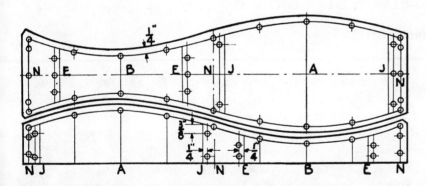

3 PATTERNS WITH HOLES FOR SPLITTERS

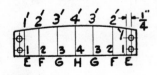

4 SPLITTERS 1 & 7

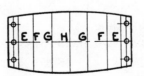

6 SPLITTERS 3 & 5

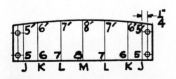

5 SPLITTERS 2 & 8

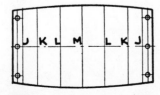

7 SPLITTERS 4 & 6

PLATE 25   OBLONG ELBOW STRAIGHT ON SIDE

This type of elbow may be laid out by drawing the first segment as in Figure 1, which is the same method used for any other round elbow. If the quarter-pattern method is to be used, then it is not necessary to draw the $2\frac{1}{2}$-in. times 4-in. oblong front profile as in Figure 1. It will be necessary only to obtain the straight between the two half circles which represent the oblong. This may be obtained by subtracting the small figure from the large which in this case is $4 - 2\frac{1}{2} = 1\frac{1}{2}$ in.

To develop the quarter pattern as in Figure 3, draw the base line to equal one quarter of the circumference of the $2\frac{1}{2}$-in. diameter circle plus half the straight between the two half circles. Transfer the height $C-D$ in Figure 1 to $C-D$ in Figure 3, and proceed as in the previous plate.

Figure 2 shows two methods of developing Pattern No. 1, the long method and the method of applying the quarter pattern.

PLATE 26   OBLONG ELBOW STRAIGHT ON

HEEL AND THROAT

Draw the first segment using the same method as for any round elbow. If the quarter pattern is to be used, then it is not necessary to draw the oblong profile as in Figure 1. It will be necessary only to obtain the straight between the two half circles by subtracting the small figure from the large as, in this case, $4 - 2\frac{1}{2} = 1\frac{1}{2}$ in.

To develop the quarter pattern as in Figure 3, draw the base line to equal half of the straight between the two half circles, plus one quarter of the circumference. Transfer the height $C-D$ from Figure 1 to $C-D$ in Figure 3. Divide the end quarter circle and the quarter circumference 7 to F into the same number of spaces. Transfer the heights 2 and 3 from the end curve to the lines 2 and 3 on line $7-F$.

Figure 2 shows two methods of developing Pattern No. 1, the long method and the method of applying the quarter pattern.

PLATE 25

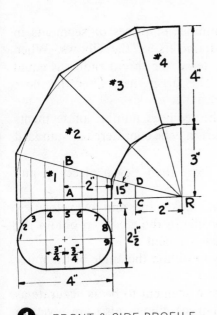

1 FRONT & SIDE PROFILE

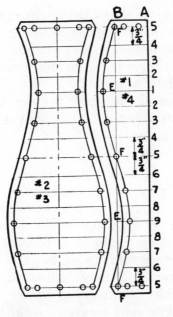

2 PATTERN FOR OBLONG ELBOW

3 ¼ PATTERN

PLATE 26

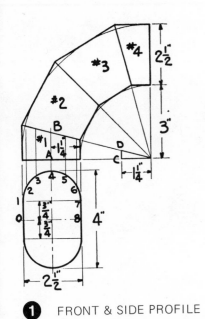

1 FRONT & SIDE PROFILE

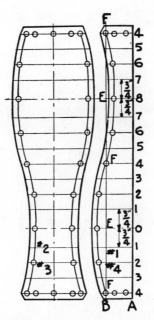

2 PATTERNS FOR OBLONG ELBOW

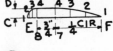

3 ¼ PATTERN

CHART 1   ROUND-ELBOW SHORT CUTS

Chart 1, following, shows the required number of pieces or segments in 90-deg. elbows in accordance with the diameters of the elbows. When elbows are used in blowpipe or exhaust systems, the throat radius is equal to one, two, or three times the diameter. The larger the radius, the more efficient the elbow will be.

NOTE: When the diameter increases, the required number of segments also increases as shown in Chart 1. This chart may be considered as standard practice in the larger shops.

It is not necessary or practical to use more than eleven pieces in any 90-deg. elbow regardless of the diameter.

Three- and four-piece elbows are used for smoke pipes and low velocities.

It is not necessary to lay out the full profile of the elbow to obtain the angle or the rise of the miter line for the first segment.

Chart 2 gives the rise in 24 in. necessary to obtain the angle of the miter line for the first segment in various elbows.

The rises given in 24 in. will allow the first segment to be as accurate as humanly possible. The rises for 9- and 11-piece elbows also are given in 36 in. This will be more accurate for the larger diameter elbows, especially when the total of the diameter plus the radius will be many feet longer than the length of the base line of these angles.

NUMBER OF SEGMENTS FOR VARIOUS DIAMETERS

CHART 1

Diameter of Elbows	Pieces or Segments
6 in. or less	5
7 to 15 in.	7
16 to 30 in.	9
31 in. or larger	11

PLATE 27   USING ELBOW CHART 2

To use the angles in Chart 2 to lay out the first segment for an elbow, select the number of pieces or segments for the elbow from Chart 1, for example, in this case 7. Following across the page in Chart 2, from 7 in the first column to the third column, it will show that the rise in 24 in. is 3.16 or $3\frac{5}{32}$ in.

Proceed by drawing the base line 24 in. long. Then, at one end, draw a line upward equal to the height or rise of the angle as given in the third column of Chart 2 and represented by *A*, *B*, and *C* in Figure 1. This shows how the first segment may be laid out for a 7-piece elbow, with 8-in. radius and 10-in. diameter. The radius is marked from the point of the angle as *A* to *D*; the diameter then is marked as *D* to *E*, representing the first segment. The pattern now may be laid out using any method desired.

When the radius plus the diameter of the elbow total more than 24 in., the length of the base line of the angle, then both lines, the base and the slant angle line, may be continued and drawn as long as may be desired, and still maintain the correct angle, as shown in Figure 2. The radius *A* to *D* is 18 in., and the diameter *D* to *E*, 15 in.

When using the quarter-pattern method for laying out the first segment, the radius length is marked only on the base line, and a line representing half the diameter is drawn upward as in Figure 3. Proceed by using the same method as illustrated in the quarter pattern for round elbows in Plate 21. Using Chart 2 as a reference guide will save many hours of labor.

PLATE 28   ELBOW CHART 2. RISES IN 24 IN. FOR FIRST SEGMENTS

Pieces or Segments in Elbow	Deg. or Angle of First Segment	
3	22.50	22.50° — 24" — 9.94" OR $9\frac{15}{16}$"
4	15	15° — 24" — 6.43" OR $6\frac{7}{16}$"
5	11.25	11.25° — 24" — 4.77" OR $4\frac{25}{32}$"
6	9	9° — 24" — 3.80" OR $3\frac{13}{16}$"
7	7.50	7.50° — 24" — 3.16" OR $3\frac{5}{32}$"

PLATE 27

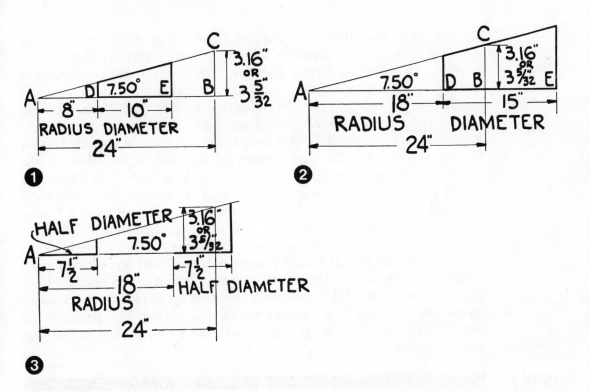

①

②

③

PLATE 28

Pieces or Segments in Elbow	Deg. or Angle of First Segment.	
9	5.625	5.625° — 24" — 2.36" OR 2⅜"
10	5	5° — 24" — 2.099" OR 2³⁄₃₂"
11	4.50	4.50° — 24" — 1.88" OR 1⅞"
9	5.625	5.625° — 36" — 3.54" OR 3³⁵⁄₆₄"
11	4.50	4.50° — 36" — 2.83" OR 2²⁷⁄₃₂"

39

CHART 3   OBTAINING ANGLES LESS THAN 90 DEG.

Chart 3 shows how angles of various degrees may be obtained for elbows when using the two end segments and one or more center segments.

When an angle of a certain degree is desired, follow down column 5 to the desired degree, then move to column 4 showing the number of center segments to be added to the two end segments in column 3. The figure in column 1 shows the number of segments in the elbow from which the first segment is to be taken. Refer to Chart 2 and follow down column 1 to the number representing the same number of segments in the elbow as the number in column 1 in Chart 3. Move across to column 3 in Chart 2 to obtain the rise in the first segment in 24 in. For example: A 75-deg. angle is desired. In column 5, Chart 3, move down to the line representing a 75-deg. angle; move across to column 4 to obtain the required number of center segments (in this case 4), and then move to column 1 where a 7-piece elbow is listed. Then, in Chart 2, column 1, move down to 7, and across to column 3 to obtain the rise in 24 in. for the first segment, which in this case is 3.16 or $3\frac{5}{32}$ in. Keep in mind that the center segments are always twice the width of one end segment. This example shows that the two end segments are each $7\frac{1}{2}$ deg., the four center segments are each 15 deg., and the six segments total 75 deg.

CHART 3

No. of Pieces in 90-Deg. Elbows	Deg. of First Segment	No. of End Segments	No. of Center Segments	Deg. of Angle Desired
1	2	3	4	5
4	15	2 = 30 dg.	1 = 30 deg.	60
5	11.25	2 = 22.50 deg.	1 = 22.50 deg.	45
6	9	2 = 18 deg.	3 = 54 deg.	72
7	7.50	2 = 15 deg.	1 = 15 deg.	30
7	7.50	2 = 15 deg.	2 = 30 deg.	45
7	7.50	2 = 15 deg.	3 = 45 deg.	60
7	7.50	2 = 15 deg.	4 = 60 deg.	75
9	5.625	2 = 11.25 deg.	1 = 11.25 deg.	22.50
9	5.625	2 = 11.25 deg.	3 = 33.75 deg.	45
10	5	2 = 10 deg.	1 = 10 deg.	20
10	5	2 = 10 deg.	2 = 20 deg.	30
10	5	2 = 10 deg.	3 = 30 deg.	40
10	5	2 = 10 deg.	4 = 40 deg.	50
10	5	2 = 10 deg.	5 = 50 deg.	60
10	5	2 = 10 deg.	6 = 60 deg.	70
10	5	2 = 10 deg.	7 = 70 deg.	80
11	4.50	2 = 9 deg.	4 = 36 deg.	45

SELECTING THE NUMBER OF RIVET HOLES
AS PER DIAMETER

CHART 4

The table in Chart 4 shows the number of rivet holes to be placed in various diameters of pipes, elbows, etc. This may be considered as standard practice in the larger shops.

CHART 4

Diameter of Pipe in In.	No. of Rivet Holes
2 to 4	4
5 to 9	6
10 to 16	8
17 to 23	10
24 to 30	12
31 to 39	16
40 to 50	20

PLATE 29   ROUND THREE-PIECE OFFSET

For a side profile as in Figure 1, draw a base line and mark the $2\frac{1}{2}$-in. offset and the 4-in. diameter $A-B$. Mark the 8-in. height and the 4-in. diameter at the top. Draw the heights of the throat $A-C$ and $A-G$ to the dimensions as shown.

To obtain the heights for the heel, use $A-B$ as a radius, and points C and G as centers. Strike an arc at the heel from the vertical line to an undetermined length. Then draw a straight line from point G tangent to the arc drawn and intersecting the vertical line at point D. Draw a straight line from point C tangent to the arc and intersecting the vertical line at point H. This will be the height for the heel of part 3, which is the same height as for part 1.

Draw a half circle below the profile, and project lines to intersect the slant line $C-D$ in the same manner as in previous plates. It is not necessary to project lines from part 1 into parts 2 and 3. The distances C to E and G to F in part 2 are equal to the height A to C in part 1. Transfer the height $A-C$ from points C to E and G to F. The distances D to F and H to E in part 2 are equal to the height B to D in part 1. Transfer the height $B-D$ from points D to F and H to E as shown in Figure 1.

To lay out a pattern for part 1 as in Figure 2, use the same method as described for the peening-edge elbows in previous plates. The pattern for part 3 is a duplicate of the pattern for part 1 with only a single edge.

To lay out a pattern for part 2, transfer the length E to E and F to F from the side profile in Figure 1 to lines $E-E$ and $F-F$ in Figure 2. Then place Pattern No. 1 on line $E-F$ at the top, and Pattern No. 3 on line $E-F$ at the bottom. Then draw the curved lines at the top and bottom to complete Pattern No. 2 as shown.

Figure 3 shows an assembled offset with the peening edges closed.

PLATE 29

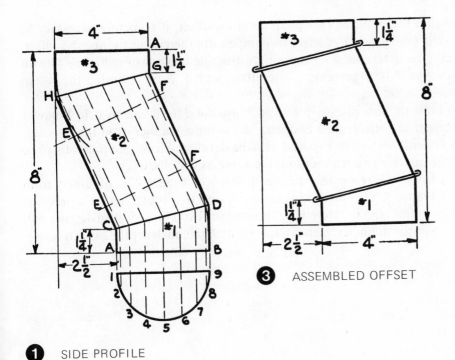

1 SIDE PROFILE

3 ASSEMBLED OFFSET

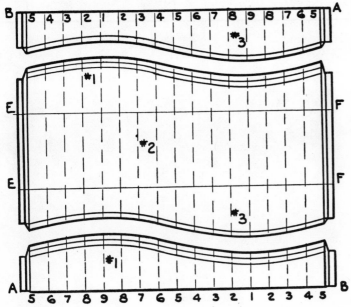

2 DEVELOPED PATTERNS WITH PEENING EDGES

PLATE 30   DOUBLE OFFSET

To develop the patterns for this type of an offset, it is merely necessary to obtain the increase in the offset to compensate the rise in the second offset. This may be determined by drawing a triangle as shown in Figure 1, with the base line $A-C$ representing one offset, and $A-B$ representing the rise in the second offset.

To draw the side profile in Figure 3, use the slant line B to C in Figure 1 to represent the offset; then continue in the same manner as in the previous plate. The full pattern in Figure 5 may be developed as in the previous plate or by the quarter-pattern method, the same as for elbows.

The height $G-H$ on the quarter pattern in Figure 4 is obtained from $G-H$ in Figure 3. This method is identical with that illustrated in a previous plate for round elbows. Here we eliminate the extra step of transferring half the width of the diameter to the radius point R to construct the same triangle.

PLATE 30

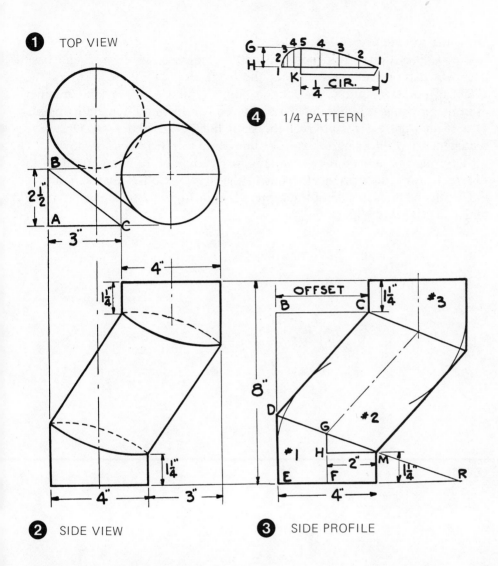

1 TOP VIEW

4 1/4 PATTERN

2 SIDE VIEW

3 SIDE PROFILE

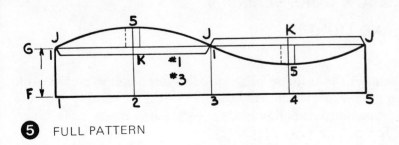

5 FULL PATTERN

PLATE 31   COMPOUND OBLONG OFFSET

Draw the top view as in Figure 1.

Draw lines down from points 3 and 12 intersecting the top and base lines which represent the height of the front view in Figure 2. Mark the height of points D and E, and obtain points C and F in the same manner as in the previous offset plates. Draw lines down from the remaining points 1 to 18 in Figure 1 to intersect the slant lines C–D and E–F. Draw the center line A–B crossing the various lines, and number each as shown.

Lay out the end pattern as in Figure 3, and the center pattern as in Figure 4, using the same method as in the previous offset plates. Transfer the widths from each side of the center A–B in Figure 2 to each side of the center line A–B in Figure 4.

PLATE 32   WELDING ELBOW GORE SEAMS

18 GAUGE AND LIGHTER

This plate illustrates the forming of seam edges for welding elbows with smooth overlapping seams which will add strength to the seams.

The preparation and seam allowance for each gore section is illustrated and explained in detail on Plate 23.

When the duct continues from the elbow and the seams welded, then the same $\frac{1}{8}$ inch allowance is made at the end of each end gore. The small end will be offset or shrunk in the same manner as the center gore.

NOTE: When assembling and aligning of gore sections, the first tack weld must be made at center of heel or back of elbow. This will facilitate the aligning of the throat to the required degree for that portion or segment of elbow. Tack weld each side before completing weld.

PLATE 31

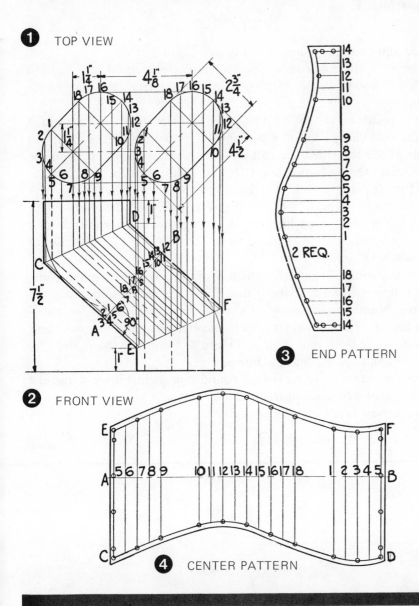

1 TOP VIEW

2 FRONT VIEW

3 END PATTERN

2 REQ.

4 CENTER PATTERN

PLATE 32

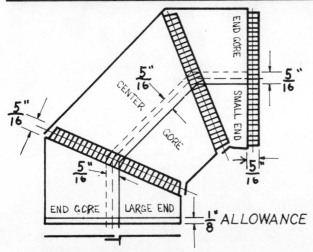

END GORE

SMALL END

CENTER GORE

$\frac{5}{16}''$

END GORE   LARGE END

$\frac{1}{8}''$ ALLOWANCE

PLATE 33   ROUND T INTERSECTING A ROUND PIPE AT A 90-DEG. ANGLE

Draw the side and end views shown in Figures 1 and 2.

Divide the half circle above each view into eight equal spaces, and number each as shown. Project straight lines down from the half circle above the end view to intersect the round pipe. Project straight lines from the intersecting points on the round pipe in the end view to an undetermined length into the side view. Project a straight line down from each point on the half circle above the side view to intersect the lines projected from the end view, to obtain the V-shaped line 1 to 5 to 9 shown in the side view.

NOTE: After drawing line 1 to 1 equal to the circumference, lay out only one quarter of the T pattern as 1 to 5 in Figure 3. Add the riveting lap. Then cut out along the curved line 1 to 5. Using this quarter cutout as a template, trace the curved cutting line 5 to 9, 9 to 5, and 5 to 1. The use of this method will save time.

To lay out the round T pattern shown in Figure 3, stretch out the circumference on line A–B, and divide it into equal spaces the same as in the previous plates. Number each point as shown. Take the heights for the T pattern from line A–B to the round pipe in the end view, and transfer these heights to points 1 to 9 on line A–B in Figure 3. Complete the pattern by drawing the freehand curved line as shown.

To lay out the cutout opening on the round pipe as in Figure 4, use the same method as that described in the previous plates.

An isometric view is shown in Figure 5.

PLATE 33

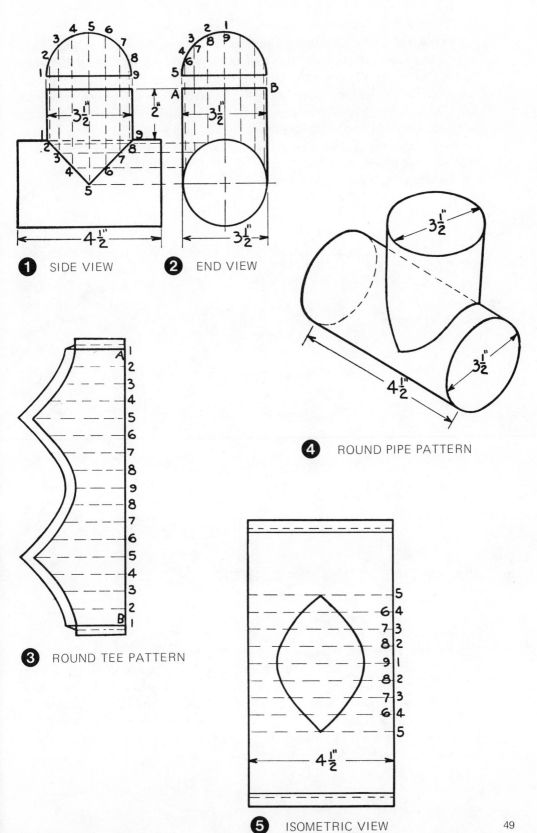

1 SIDE VIEW

2 END VIEW

3 ROUND TEE PATTERN

4 ROUND PIPE PATTERN

5 ISOMETRIC VIEW

49

PLATE 34 ROUND T INTERSECTING A ROUND PIPE AT A 90-DEG. ANGLE OFF CENTER

Draw the side and end views shown in Figures 1 and 2.

Divide the half circles into equal spaces and number each as shown.

Project lines down from the half circle above each view in the same manner as in the previous plates. Then project lines from the end view to the side view. Care must be observed so that each line from the end view will intersect its corresponding numbered line in the side view to obtain the freehand curved line shown in Figure 1.

To lay out the T and pipe patterns, use the same method described in the previous plates.

An isometric view is shown in Figure 5.

PLATE 35 ROUND T AT 90 DEG. ON CENTER

Use the short method to draw the T profile, then draw the side view of T. Use one half the diameter of the large pipe to draw the arc $A-B$. Draw lines 2, 3, and 4 down into pipe profile. Transfer the distance 1 to E from the T to one or both ends of pipe as shown 1 to E, then transfer the distance D to $2'$, and C to $3'$ from the T to the ends of the pipe as shown $C3'$ and $D2'$. Draw lines crossing the lines drawn down from the T and obtain the T intersection to layout the T pattern.

PLATE 34

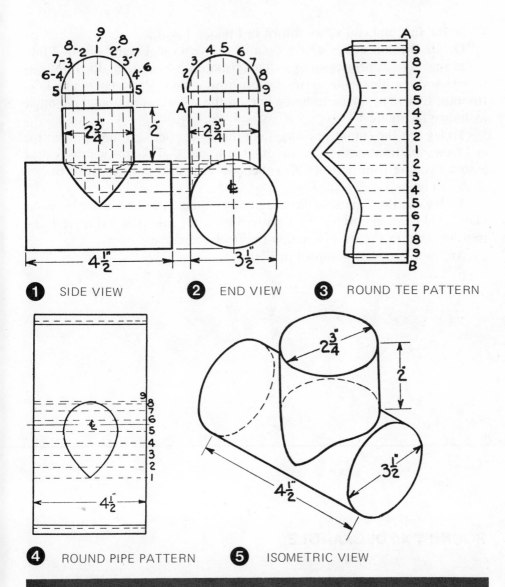

1 SIDE VIEW

2 END VIEW

3 ROUND TEE PATTERN

4 ROUND PIPE PATTERN

5 ISOMETRIC VIEW

PLATE 35

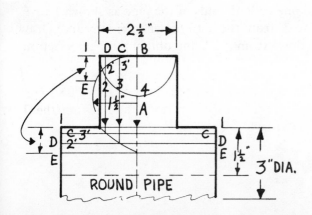

ROUND PIPE

3" DIA.

Draw the side and end views shown in Figures 1 and 2.

Divide the half circles above each of the views in Figures 1 and 2 into equal spaces, and project straight lines from each half circle down into its respective view the same as in the previous plates. Project straight lines from the end view, intersecting the lines in the side view, to obtain the angle as shown in Figure 1.

To lay out the cutout opening, take the spaces on the round pipe in the end view, and transfer them to line A–B in Figure 3. Take the widths for the cutout opening from line A–B in the side view and transfer them to line A–B in Figure 3.

To lay out the T pattern use the same method described in the previous plates. Take the lengths for the T pattern from the side view in Figure 1 and transfer them to Figure 4 to obtain the freehand curve shown.

An isometric view is shown in Figure 5.

PLATE 37   ROUND T 45 DEG. ANGLE

Short method to draw the T profile. Draw the side view of the T. Use one half of the diameter of the large pipe to draw the arc A–B. Transfer the distance 1 to E from the T to one or both ends of the pipe as shown 1 to E, also transfer D to 2′, and C to 3′ from the T to the ends of the pipe. Draw lines crossing the lines drawn down from the T and obtain the T intersection.

PLATE 36

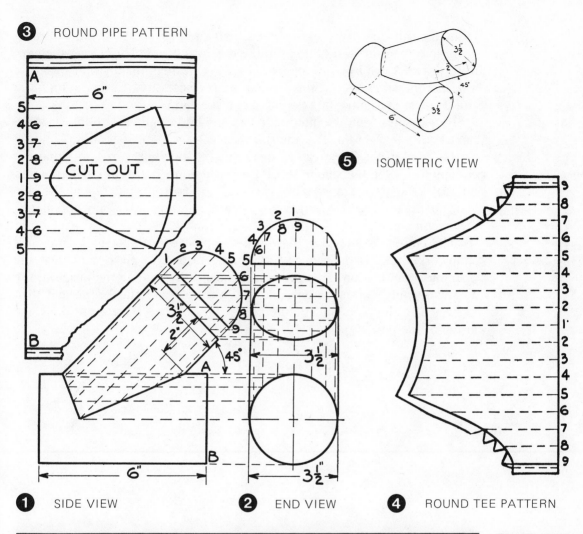

③ ROUND PIPE PATTERN

⑤ ISOMETRIC VIEW

① SIDE VIEW

② END VIEW

④ ROUND TEE PATTERN

PLATE 37

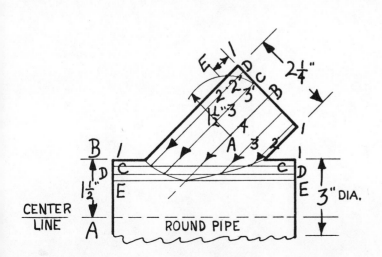

CENTER LINE

ROUND PIPE

$2\frac{1}{4}$"

$1\frac{1}{2}$"

3" DIA.

PLATE 38   ROUND T INTERSECTING PIPE AT A 45-DEG.
ANGLE OFF CENTER

Draw the end view as in Figure 2. The half circle on the T should be drawn down into the T instead of up as in the previous plates. This allows the lines to be drawn down by squaring from line 4–4 through the division spaces to intersect the large circle, thus eliminating the necessity of using a T square and triangle that may not be available in the shop.

Project lines from the intersection points in the end view to intersect the slant lines 1 to 7 on the T in the side view.

To develop the T pattern as in Figure 3, draw line 1 to 1 to equal the circumference of the diameter of the T, and divide it into the required number of spaces. Transfer the various lengths from line 1–7 in the side view to their respective lengths in Figure 3. Allow for seam and flange for riveting.

The cutout opening for the T on the pipe is not shown. In practical shopwork the T is flanged and set on its respective place, and then the opening is marked on the pipe with a pencil drawn along the inside of the T. The opening then is cut out, and the rivet holes are punched. The T then is riveted to the pipe, and the notched edges on the T are bent along the inside of the pipe.

PLATE 38

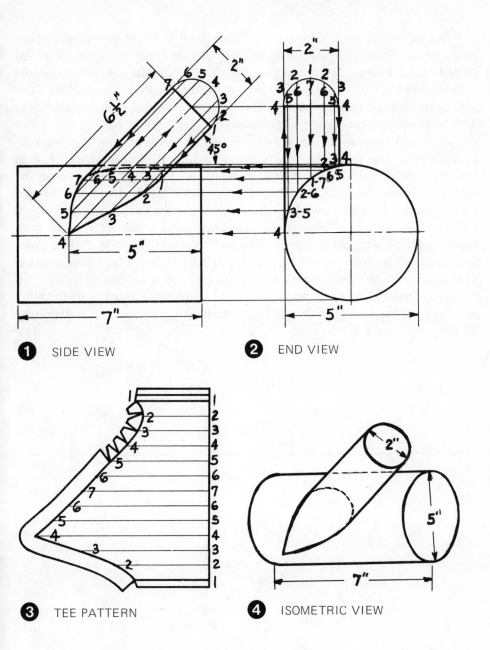

1 SIDE VIEW

2 END VIEW

3 TEE PATTERN

4 ISOMETRIC VIEW

PLATE 39 DOUBLE-ANGLE ROUND T, 45-DEG.

DEFLECTING 30 DEG.

A T of this type is used when it is at a certain angle in the side or plan view (such as the 45-deg. angle in Fig. 1) and the trunk line is turned or rolled to deflect the T from its normal position. The deflection points up or down a certain number of degrees (such as the 30 deg. illustrated in the end view Fig. 2) to clear or pass an object or an obstruction that may not allow the T to be in an upright or a level position.

To obtain the proper angle (49 deg. in this problem) for the working profile so that the T pattern may be developed, draw the center line $A-B$ in the side view, Figure 1, equal to the angle of the T as may be shown on the plan (in this problem 45 deg.) and the length of the T. Draw the 30-deg. center line in the end view, Figure 2; this represents the angle that the T must be turned to pass an obstruction. Then draw a line from point B to intersect the 30-deg. center line in Figure 2 to establish point D. Use point C as a center to draw an arc from point D to E; draw a line from point E to intersect the center line drawn up from point B, establishing point F in Figure 2. Draw a line from point F to point A on the center line of the pipe, thereby obtaining the new length, and the new angle for a 45 T deflecting 30 deg.

PLATE 39

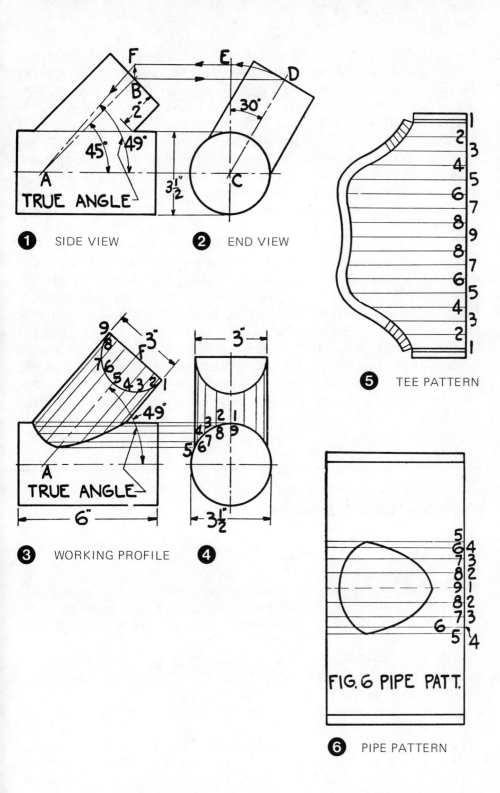

1 SIDE VIEW

TRUE ANGLE

2 END VIEW

3 WORKING PROFILE

4

5 TEE PATTERN

6 PIPE PATTERN

FIG. 6 PIPE PATT.

57

PLATE 40 45-DEG. ANGLE ELBOW ON A 45-DEG T.

DEFLECTING 30 DEG.

NOTE: The procedure for obtaining the 49-deg. angle for the T in this plate is the same as that in Plate 39; therefore, only the procedure for obtaining the true angle, or the additional degrees that may be required when the angle elbow is deflected (turned up or down) during the installation will be emphasized.

Draw the 45-deg. T, and the 45-deg. angle elbow in the side view, Figure 1. Draw the end view in Figure 2; then draw a line from point *C* in Figure 2 to intersect with the center line *B–G* on the 45-deg. angle elbow in Figure 1. Next draw a line from point *C* to point *A* at the center line of the pipe to obtain the length of the view center line, and the new 49-deg. angle for the T.

To obtain the new angle, and the new length of the center line *B–G* for the new angle elbow, draw a line down from points *A* and *B* in Figure 1 to line *A–C* in Figure 3. Then construct the triangle *A–J–B* by transferring the distance *J* to *B* from the triangle in Figure 2 to line *J–B* in Figure 3. Use point *A* as a center to draw the arc *B* to *C* and establish point *D* in Figure 1. Draw the slant solid line from point *D* to *B* representing the angle for the new angle elbow. Use the distance *H* to *G* as a radius and point *B* as a center to draw the arc *E* to *E* representing the 49-deg. angle for the new elbow. Draw a 90-deg. line from the vertical line *B–A*, and a 90-deg. line from the slant line *B–D* to intersect at point *F*, thereby establishing the length of line *E* to *F* in Figure 4, a working profile to lay out the new angle elbow patterns.

PLATE 41 75-DEG. ANGLE ELBOW DEFLECTING 30 DEG.

When an angle elbow must be deflected (be turned or rolled up or down) during the installation, a certain number of degrees must be added to the angle to maintain the proper angle in the plan and to follow the established course of travel.

Figures 1 and 2 illustrate the procedure to follow for obtaining those additional degrees to be added to a 75-deg. elbow deflecting 30-deg. (changing the angle of the elbow from 75 deg. to 77 deg.).

Draw the base line (throat radius and diameter of elbow); then draw the 75-deg. angle line *A–B* to any length desired. Now at random, establish point *C* on the base line at any place desired; then draw a 90-deg. line up from point *C* to cross the 75-deg. Angle Line *A-B*, obtaining point *D*.

Now at Figure 2 erect a 30-deg. angle as represented by points *A–B–E*. Use point *A* as a center to draw an arc from point *E* to intersect line *C–D* to obtain point *F*. Draw a line from point *F* to *A* establishing the new angle (77 deg.) or the additional degrees for a deflected angle elbow. Continue the throat and heel curve to the new angle line.

PLATE 40

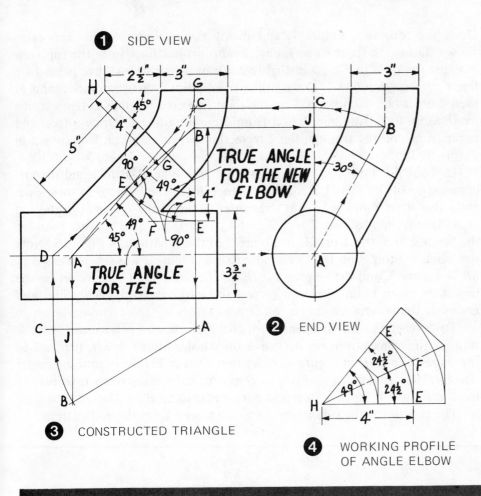

1 SIDE VIEW

TRUE ANGLE FOR THE NEW ELBOW

TRUE ANGLE FOR TEE

3 CONSTRUCTED TRIANGLE

2 END VIEW

4 WORKING PROFILE OF ANGLE ELBOW

PLATE 41

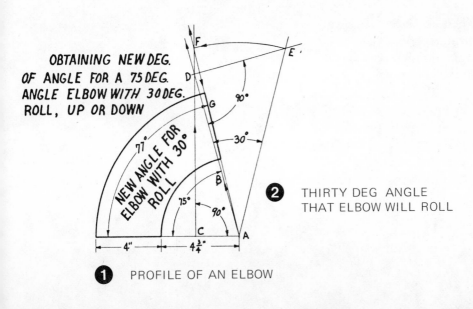

OBTAINING NEW DEG. OF ANGLE FOR A 75 DEG. ANGLE ELBOW WITH 30 DEG. ROLL, UP OR DOWN

NEW ANGLE FOR ELBOW WITH 30° ROLL

2 THIRTY DEG ANGLE THAT ELBOW WILL ROLL

1 PROFILE OF AN ELBOW

PLATE 42   ROUND T INTERSECTING A HOOD AT THE HIP

Draw the top view, Figure 1, and divide the circle into equal spaces as shown. Draw the front view, Figure 2, and project lines from the top view crossing the slant line *C–D* in Figure 2. Draw a line across from point 1 on line *C–D* crossing line 4. Draw a line from point 2 crossing lines 3 and 5; then draw a line from point 3 on the slant line crossing line 6. Draw a line from point 4 crossing line 7, and from 5 crossing line 6. Draw a freehand curve from point *A* through the intersecting points to point *B* as shown in Figure 2.

Lay out the T pattern as in Figure 3. Draw line *B–B* to equal the circumference of the T, and mark the distance *B* to 5 and *B* to 6 in from each end; also *A* to 2 and *A* to 3 at the center to equal those spaces in the top view. Divide the distance 2 to 5*B* and 3 to 6*B* into equal spaces. Transfer the heights from the T profile in Figure 2 to the T pattern in Figure 3. Note the heights 3 to 6*B* on the freehand curve in Figure 2 are set on lines 3 to 6*B* in Figure 3, and the heights 1 to *B* on the slant line *C–D* are set on the line *A* to 5*B* in Figure 3. Draw a freehand curve through each point, and complete the pattern as shown.

To develop the cutout opening for the T on the end pattern in Figure 4, transfer the spaces from point *C* to *B* on the slant line *C–D* in Figure 2 to the center line *C–D* in Figure 4. Pick the widths in Figure 1 from the center line *E–F* to the circular points 1 to *B* and transfer them to their respective lines in Figure 4. Draw a freehand curve from *A* to *B*.

The cutout for the side pattern may be traced from the end pattern.

PLATE 42

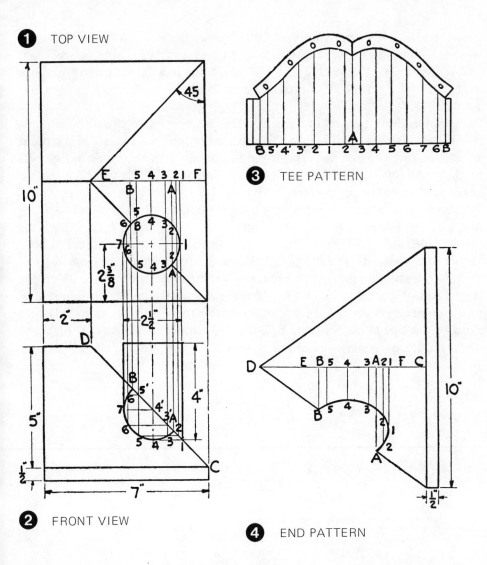

① TOP VIEW

③ TEE PATTERN

② FRONT VIEW

④ END PATTERN

PLATE 43   ROUND T INTERSECTING A HOOD

AT THE RIDGE AND HIPS

Draw the top view and front view and project the line 1 to 7 from the top view, crossing lines $C-D$ and $A-D$ in Figure 2. Draw a line across from point 7 on line $C-D$ crossing line 4. Draw a line from point 6 crossing lines 3 and 5, and from point 2 crossing line 2. Draw a freehand curve from 1 to B.

Develop the T pattern in Figure 3. Draw line $A-A$ to equal the circumference of the T and divide into the required number of spaces. Mark point B between points 5 and 6. Transfer the heights from the T profile in Figure 2 to their respective lines on the T pattern in Figure 3. Draw the freehand curve and complete the pattern as shown.

To lay out the end pattern in Figure 4, transfer the spaces C to B on line $C-D$ in Figure 2 to the center line $C-D$ in Figure 4. Pick the widths from either side of the center line 1–7 in Figure 1, and transfer them to both sides of the center $C-D$ in Figure 4. Draw the freehand curve from B to B.

Lay out the side pattern in Figure 5. Transfer the spaces C to D on the slant line in Figure 2 to line $C-D$ in Figure 5. Pick the widths from line $1-E$ to the circular points in Figure 1, and transfer them to their respective lines drawn from line $C-D$ in Figure 5. Draw a freehand curve from A to B, and allow for seams as may be desired.

PLATE 43

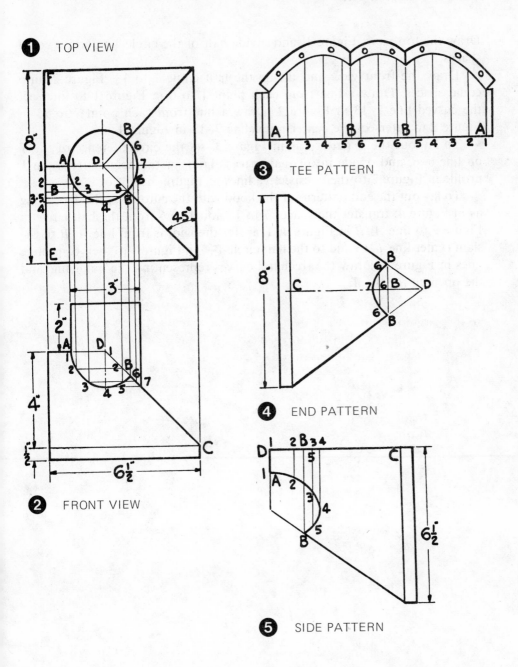

① TOP VIEW

② FRONT VIEW

③ TEE PATTERN

④ END PATTERN

⑤ SIDE PATTERN

PLATE 44   CYLINDER INTERSECTING A QUARTER-ROUND
HOOD AT THE HIP

Draw the top view, Figure 1, and divide half of the circle 1 to 6 into equal spaces.

Draw the front view and divide the half circle 7 to 13, Figure 2, into equal spaces. Draw a line from each point 1 to 6 in Figure 1 to intersect the curved line 7–13 in Figure 2. Draw a line from each point 7 to 13 in Figure 2 to intersect the center miter line 7–13 in Figure 1.

To lay out the T pattern as in Figure 3, set the circumference of the T on line 6–6, and divide into equal spaces. Transfer the heights from the T profile in Figure 2 to their respective lines in Figure 3.

To lay out the end pattern for the hood with the cutout for the T opening as in Figure 4, transfer the spaces 7 to 13 and 1 to 6 from the half circle in Figure 2 to line $A-B$ in Figure 4. Transfer the widths from line $A-B$ to the slant center line 7–13 and to the half circle 1–6 in Figure 1 to their respective lines in Figure 4. Draw the freehand curves representing the miter line and the opening for the T.

PLATE 44

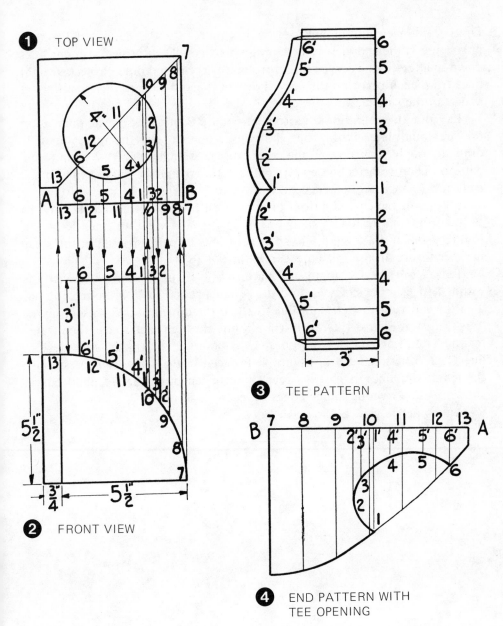

1 TOP VIEW

2 FRONT VIEW

3 TEE PATTERN

4 END PATTERN WITH TEE OPENING

PLATE 45 **RECTANGULAR T INTERSECTING A ROUND PIPE AT A 45-DEG. ANGLE ON CENTER**

Draw a side view and an end view as in Figures 1 and 2. Divide the rectangular pipe in the end view into four equal spaces. Then project straight lines down to intersect the curved line representing the round pipe. Project straight lines from each point on the curved line in the end view to intersect lines *A* and *B* in the side view.

Lay out the round-pipe pattern in Figure 3 in the same manner as in the previous plate. To lay out the cutout opening for the rectangular T, draw a straight line through the center of the stretchout for the round-pipe pattern. Then transfer the equal spaces 1 to 3 from the curved line in the end view to each side of the center line 1 to 3 in Figure 3.

To obtain the curved cutout lines *A–B* in Figure 3, transfer the lengths 1–2–3 from line *C* to the slant line *B* in the side view, to lines 1–2–3 in Figure 3. Then draw the freehand curved line *B* to *B*. Proceed in the same manner to obtain the freehand curved line *A* to *A*.

To lay out the rectangular T pattern shown in Figure 4, transfer the width *A* to *B* in the side view and the equal spaces 3 to 3 on the rectangular T in the end view to a straight line to equal the dimensions representing the T as shown in Figure 4. Draw a straight line through each space, then transfer the lengths for the T from point *B* to points 1, 2, 3 in the side view, to lines 1, 2, 3 between *BB* in Figure 4. Proceed in the same way to establish the lengths of lines 1, 2, 3 between *A–A*. Then draw the freehand curves shown. Allow riveting flange edges on each as shown.

An isometric view is shown in Figure 5.

PLATE 45

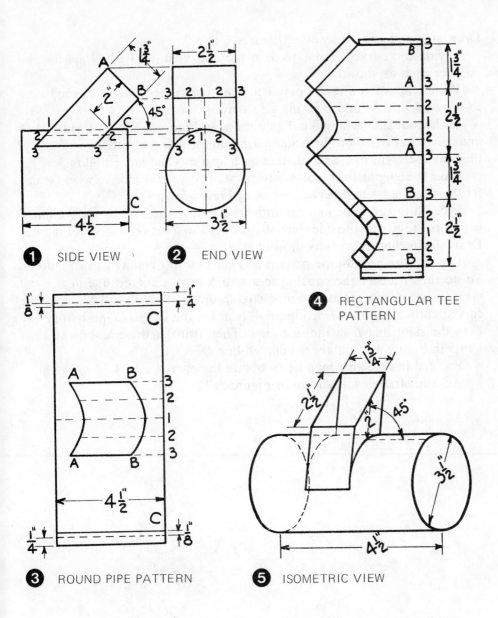

1 SIDE VIEW

2 END VIEW

4 RECTANGULAR TEE PATTERN

3 ROUND PIPE PATTERN

5 ISOMETRIC VIEW

Draw side and end views as in Figures 1 and 2.

Divide the curved line 1 to 5 in the end view into equal spaces and number each as shown.

Project lines from each point 1 to 5 on the curved line in the end view to intersect lines *A* and *B* in the side view.

To lay out the rectangular T pattern as in Figure 3, take the width *A–B* and the spaces 1 to 5 on the rectangular T in the side and end views, transfer them to a straight line, and number each space as shown in Figure 3.

Take the lengths from point *A* to points 1 to 5 in the side view and transfer them to lines 1 to 5 between *A–A* in Figure 3.

Proceed in the same manner with transferring the lengths from point *B* to points 1 to 5 from the side view, to the lines 1 to 5 between *B–B* in Figure 3. Draw the freehand curves as shown.

Lay out the round-pipe pattern and the cutout opening as in Figure 4. To do this, transfer the equal spaces 1 to 5 on the curved line in the end view to line *C* on the round-pipe stretch-out in Figure 4. To obtain the curved cutout lines *A–B* in Figure 4, transfer the lengths 1 to 5 from line *C* to the slant line *B* in the side view. Then transfer these lengths to lines 1 to 5 in Figure 4 to obtain the curved line *B–B*.

Proceed in the same manner to obtain the curved line *A–A*.

An isometric view is shown in Figure 5.

PLATE 46

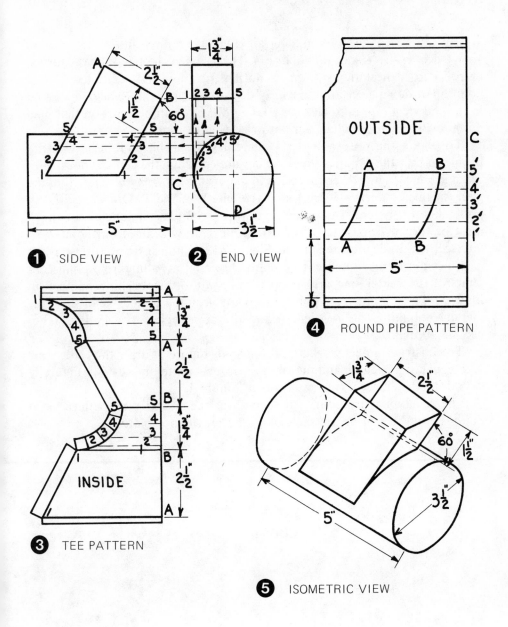

1 SIDE VIEW

2 END VIEW

3 TEE PATTERN

INSIDE

4 ROUND PIPE PATTERN

OUTSIDE

5 ISOMETRIC VIEW

PLATE 47 **DOUBLE-ANGLE RECTANGULAR T**

45 DEG. DEFLECTING 30 DEG.

A T of this type is used when a certain angle is required in the side or plan view (such as the 45-deg. angle in Fig. 1) but when the trunk line is turned or rolled to deflect the T from its normal position. The deflected T may point up or down a certain number of degrees (such as the 30 deg. illustrated in the end view Fig. 2) to clear or pass an object or an obstruction that may not allow the T to be in an upright or a level position.

To obtain the proper angle (49 deg. in this problem) for the working profile so that the T pattern may be developed, draw the center line $A-B$ in the side view, Figure 1, equal to the angle of the T as may be shown on the plan (in this problem 45 deg.), and the length of the T. Draw the 30-deg. center line in the end view, Figure 2; this represents the angle that the T must be turned to pass an obstruction. Next draw a line from point B to intersect the 30-deg. center line in Figure 2 to establish point D. Use point C as a center to draw an arc from point D to E; draw a line from point E to intersect the center line drawn up from point B, establishing point F in Figure 2. Draw a line from point F to point A on the center line of the pipe, thereby obtaining the new length and the new angle for a 45-deg. T deflecting 30 deg.

To construct a new working profile as in Figure 3, draw the center line $A-F$ equal to the length and the angle of the new center line $A-F$ in Figure 1; then draw the end working profile as in Figure 4.

The remaining procedure for laying out the T and pipe pattern as in Figures 5 and 6 will be the same as in the previous T plates.

PLATE 47

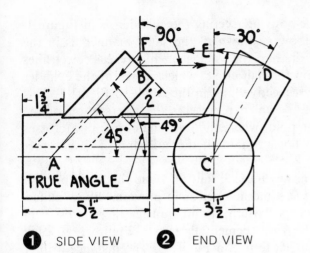

① SIDE VIEW   **②** END VIEW

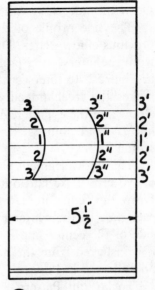

⑥ PIPE PATTERN

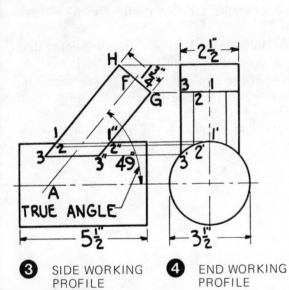

③ SIDE WORKING PROFILE   **④** END WORKING PROFILE

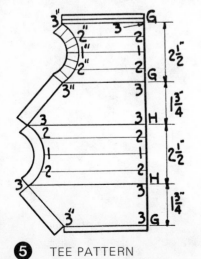

⑤ TEE PATTERN

71

PLATE 48   ELBOW INTERSECTING CYLINDER
OF LARGER DIAMETER

Draw the side view with the elbow intersecting the cylinder as in Figure 1.

The side profile of the elbow is drawn in the same manner as in the previous elbow plates. Draw the half-top view as in Figure 2. Project lines from the intersecting points on the half circle, which represent the cylinder in Figure 2, to intersect their respective lines in the elbow in Figure 1. This makes the freehand curve 1″–7′ which represents the intersection of the elbow and the cylinder. At the point where the freehand curve 1″–7′ crosses line D–D at point A, draw a line to intersect the half circle 1–7 as represented by A.

The elbow-segment patterns in Figure 3, Pattern 1 and the lower portion of Pattern 2, are laid out in the same manner as in previous elbow plates. Draw the center line B–B across Pattern 2, and transfer the widths from each side of the center line B–B on segment Pattern 2, Figure 1, to each side of the center line B–B on Pattern 2 in Figure 3. The distance 4 to A is transferred from the half circle in Figure 1 to the center line B–B from point 4 to A in Pattern 2, Figure 3.

To lay out Pattern 3, transfer the spaces 1 to A from the center line B–B on Pattern 2, to each side of point 1 to A on line C–C in Pattern 3. Transfer the widths from each side of the center line C–C on segment 3 in Figure 1, to each side of the center line C–C on Pattern 3 in Figure 3. One-quarter pattern may be used for the elbow T.

Complete the patterns by making allowances for riveting laps as shown.

PLATE 48

② HALF TOP VIEW

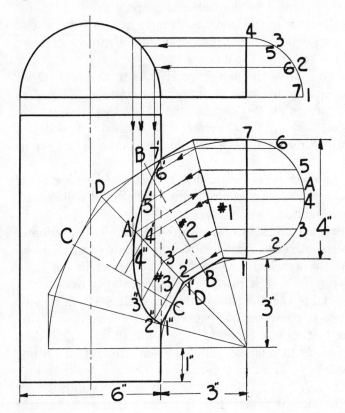

① SIDE VIEW OF ELBOW
INTERSECTING CYLINDER

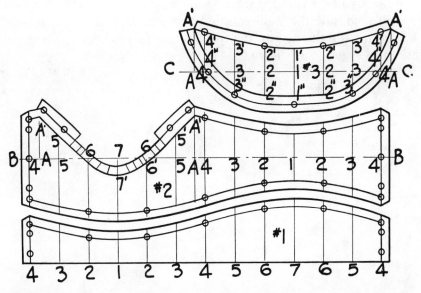

③ ELBOW SEGMENT

PLATE 49   VERTICAL T ON FIVE-PIECE ELBOW

Following are two methods of obtaining the intersecting points of the T at the back of the elbow represented by the freehand curve 5′ to 5E, Figure 1.

Draw a five-piece elbow as in the side view, Figure 1. Draw the T, and divide the half circle into equal spaces; then draw a straight line through each point until the lines pass into the elbow.

Using the first method, draw the half-front view as in Figure 2. Draw straight lines from the intersecting points on the large circle in Figure 2 to intersect the first segment line D–D. Continue these lines by drawing them parallel to the slant heel lines until they intersect their respective lines drawn down from the T. Draw a freehand curve through those intersecting points from 5 to 5E.

This method may be used conveniently if a T square and triangles are available, but in a shop which has a square but no triangles, it will be necessary to use a different method.

A second and more practical method is shown in Figure 1. It eliminates drawing Figure 2. Use point A as a center, and draw an arc or circle equal to the diameter of the elbow, which is 5 in. Draw the center line R–A to intersect the heel line at point 5. Use this point 5 as a center to draw a half circle into the elbow equal to the diameter of the T, which is $3\frac{1}{2}$ in. Divide this half circle into the same number of spaces as lines drawn down from the T. Set a square on the heel line 1–9, and draw a line through each division point on the half circle to intersect the large 5-in. circle. Draw a line through these intersecting points 4 and 6 parallel to the slant heel line 1–9, also through points 3 and 7, 2 and 8, 1 and 9 to intersect the slant segment lines B and C. Continue drawing lines 2, 3, 4, and 6 parallel to the slant heel line to intersect lines 2, 3, 4, and 6 drawn down from the T. Draw a freehand curve through the intersecting points from 5 to 5E as shown.

Lay out the T pattern as in Figure 3. Draw line 5–5 to equal the circumference and divide it into the required number of spaces. Pick the heights in Figure 1 from the top line 5–5 to the freehand curve and transfer them to the T pattern in Figure 3 as shown.

PLATE 49

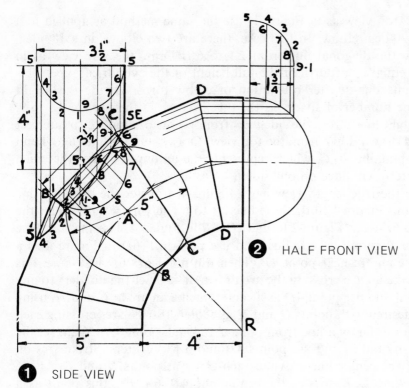

1 SIDE VIEW

2 HALF FRONT VIEW

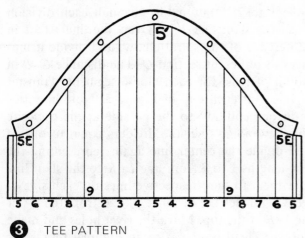

3 TEE PATTERN

PLATE 50   **SPIRAL ELBOW ENCIRCLING A CYLINDER AT TWO REVOLUTIONS**

To draw the top view as in Figure 1, use the same method as applied to a three-piece 90-deg. elbow. In this case, there are two elbows in a 180-deg. circle. Draw the diagonal line from $2A$ to $6A$. Draw the side view as in Figure 2 to equal one fourth of the full height of the cylindrical pipe. This also represents one-quarter revolution of elbow turns. Divide the height into the same number of spaces as the throat curve in the top view 1 to 9. Draw a straight line across the side view from points $6E$ and $4E$ to intersect lines 6 and 4 drawn down from the top view. Draw the slant lines 6 to 4 and $6D$ to $4D$ obtaining $B-C$, which represents the amount of twist that each segment pattern will have on one side.

To draw the true-length view as in Figure 4, transfer the diagonal line $2A$ to $6A$ from Figure 1 to the base line $2A$ to $6A$ in Figure 4. Transfer the height $2E$ to $6E$ from Figure 2 to line $2E-6E$ in Figure 4. Use the slant line $4D$ to $6D$ in Figure 2 as a radius, and use point $6A-6D$ in Figure 4 as a center. Strike an arc near point $4D$. Then use point $6E-6D$ in Figure 4 as a center. Strike an arc crossing the arc drawn at $4D$. Set the dividers to any radius desired and use point $4D$ as a center. Strike an arc at G and H, using any radius desired with points G and H as centers. Strike arcs crossing each other at point J. Draw a line from point J through point $4D$. Again set the dividers to any radius and use points $4D$ and $6A$ as centers. Strike arcs on each side of the center line crossing each other at points K and L. At the point where line $L-K$ crosses the center line $4D-6A$, use this point as a center to draw the half circle 1 to 7. Draw a line through each division point on the circle to intersect the slant line $J-N$. Draw the line 1 to 1 in Figure 3 equal to the circumference of the spiral elbow, and divide it into the required number of spaces to represent section O. The distance $C-B$ in Figure 3 represents the amount of twist for each elbow segment. Transfer this distance to one side of line 1 at each end in Figure 3. Note how this distance is set to the inside at one end and to the outside at the opposite end as marked $B-C$. On this new point 1 set the dividers equal to one of the spaces for section O and divide the center line again representing the spaces for section P. Pick the lengths 1 to 7 from line $L-K$ to the slant line $J-N$ in Figure 4, and transfer them to their respective lines on each side of the center line 1–1 in Figure 3. Transfer the distance 1 to B from the lower portion of the pattern to line 1–B at the top. Mark the rivet holes and make allowances for riveting as shown. The distance $M-N$ in Figure 4 represents the height $M-N$ on the quarter pattern in Figure 6. Line $M-M$ drawn through the pattern in Figure 3 represents the line where the base of the quarter pattern will rest to draw the curve on the pattern. This will save time in developing the segment pattern. Section O will represent one end pattern. Section P will represent the other end.

PLATE 50

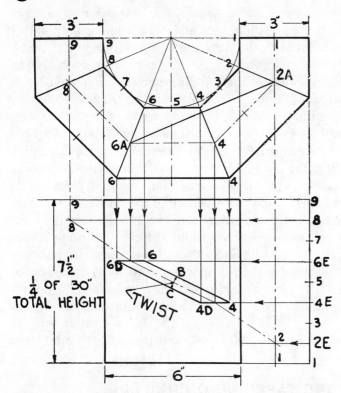

1 TOP VIEW

2 SIDE VIEW

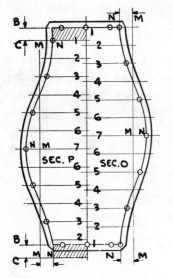

3 PATTERN

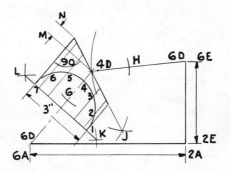

4 TRUE LENGTH VIEW

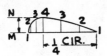

5 1/4 PATTERN

PLATE 51 ## OBLONG-TO-ROUND TAPERING ON ONE SIDE

Draw the front view in Figure 1 and scribe a quarter circle at the top. Divide the circle into three equal spaces and draw straight lines down to intersect line 1–4. Set a square on the slant line 1–*A* and draw a line from points 2, 3, and 4 on the top line to intersect the slant line 1–*A* as shown at 2, 3, and 4.

To lay out the pattern as in Figure 3, draw the top and base lines to equal one quarter of the circumference of the top diameter. Transfer the triangle 1–*B*–*A* from the front view Figure 1 to construct the triangle 1–*B*–*A* in Figure 3. Extend the slant line 1–*A* past the base line *B*–*A*. Pick the spaces 1 to 4 on the slant line 1–*A* in Figure 1, and transfer them to the slant line 1–*A* at the top and bottom in Figure 3. Number each and draw a line squaring out from each point at the top and bottom. Set the dividers to equal one of the spaces on the one-quarter circumference line. Set one point of the dividers on point 1, and then swing the other leg of the dividers so that the point strikes line 2. Keep that point resting on line 2 and swing the other leg of the dividers so that the point strikes line 3. Keep that point resting on point 3 and swing the dividers again so that the other leg strikes line 4. Draw a freehand curve crossing the pin marks put in by the dividers on lines 2, 3, and 4. Keep the dividers set and repeat the operation at the bottom of the pattern to obtain the curve 1 to 4. Time may be saved by laying out only a half pattern.

Lay out the round collar as in Figure 4, and the oblong collar as in Figure 5.

PLATE 52   OBLONG-TO-OBLONG TAPERING ON ONE SIDE

Draw the front view, Figure 1. Draw the quarter circle and follow the same procedure as in the previous plate. Lay out the pattern as in Figure 3, using the same method as in the previous plate to obtain the curve 1 to 4 at the top and the bottom. Lay out the top and bottom collars as in Figures 4 and 5.

PLATE 51

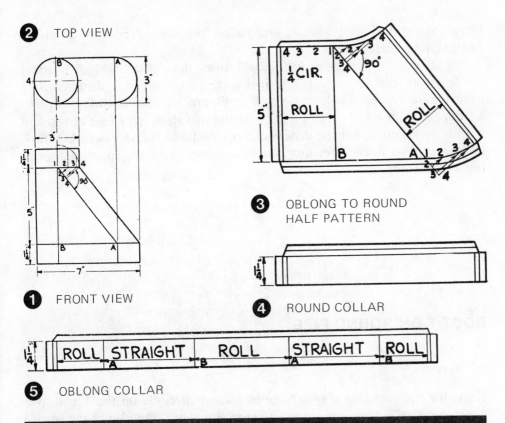

2 TOP VIEW

¼ CIR.

ROLL

ROLL

90°

5"

B

A 1 2 3 4

3 OBLONG TO ROUND
HALF PATTERN

1 FRONT VIEW

3"

4

1¼

1 2 3 4

90°

5

B A

1¼

7"

1¼

4 ROUND COLLAR

1¼ ROLL STRAIGHT A ROLL B STRAIGHT A ROLL B

5 OBLONG COLLAR

PLATE 52

2 TOP VIEW

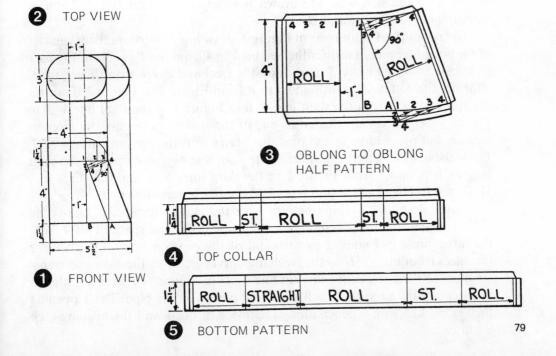

1"

3"

4 3 2 1

ROLL

1"

ROLL

90°

4"

B A 1 2 3 4

3 OBLONG TO OBLONG
HALF PATTERN

1 FRONT VIEW

4"

1¼

1 2 3 4

90°

4

B A

1½

5½"

1¼ ROLL ST. ROLL ST. ROLL

4 TOP COLLAR

1¼ ROLL STRAIGHT ROLL ST. ROLL

5 BOTTOM PATTERN

79

PLATE 53   **OBLONG-TO-ROUND TAPERING ON BOTH SIDES**

Draw the front view, Figure 1, and follow the same procedure as in the two previous plates.

To lay out the pattern as in Figure 3, draw the center line 1–B to equal the length of the center line 1–B in Figure 1. Transfer the distance B–A from Figure 1 to each side of point B in Figure 3. Transfer the spaces 1 to 4 from the slant line 1–A in Figure 1 to the two slant lines 1–A at top and bottom in Figure 3. Set the dividers to equal one of the spaces in Figure 4, and proceed as in the previous plates by stepping off the spaces 1 to 4 at top and bottom.

PLATE 54   BOOT T ON ROUND PIPE

Draw the end and side views. Note how the half circle on the T is drawn down into the T. This is more practical in shopwork. One leg of the square may be set on the top horizontal and the other to pass through the division spaces on the arc. The lines then are drawn down intersecting the larger circle. Project lines 1 to 4 from the end view, Figure 2, to intersect the lines drawn down from the top of the T in the side view. Note the lines 4 to 7 on the T in the side view are drawn parallel to the slant line 7–7. Draw freehand curves 1 to A and B to 7.

To lay out the T pattern as in Figure 3, draw line 1–4 to equal one quarter of the circumference. Transfer the heights 1 to 4 from the T profile in Figure 1 to lines 1 to 4 in Figure 3, and draw the freehand curve from line 1 to A. Transfer the distances A to B and 4 to B from Figure 1 to Figure 3. Transfer the spaces 4 to 7 from the slant line 4–B in Figure 1 to the slant line 4–B in Figure 3. Set the dividers equal to one of the spaces on the quarter circumference and proceed as in the previous plates to form the top curve 4 to 7. Draw the lines 5, 6, and 7 parallel to the slant line 4–B and transfer the slant lengths 5, 6, and 7 from Figure 1 to the slant lines 5, 6, and 7 in Figure 3. Draw the freehand curve and complete the pattern as shown.

Figure 4 shows the pipe pattern with the cutout for the T. Draw line C–D to equal the full circumference; then transfer the spaces 1 to 4 from the large circle in Figure 2 to each end of the pipe on line C–D. Pick the distances from line C–D to the freehand curves 1 to 7 in Figure 1 and transfer them to their respective lines at line C–D in Figure 4. This is not always practical. In the shop the T is flanged and placed on the pipe. The T opening then is marked with a pencil along the inside of the T and the opening then is cut out.

PLATE 53

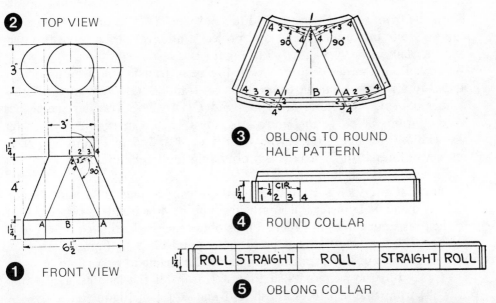

2 TOP VIEW

3 OBLONG TO ROUND HALF PATTERN

1 FRONT VIEW

4 ROUND COLLAR

5 OBLONG COLLAR

ROLL | STRAIGHT | ROLL | STRAIGHT | ROLL

PLATE 54

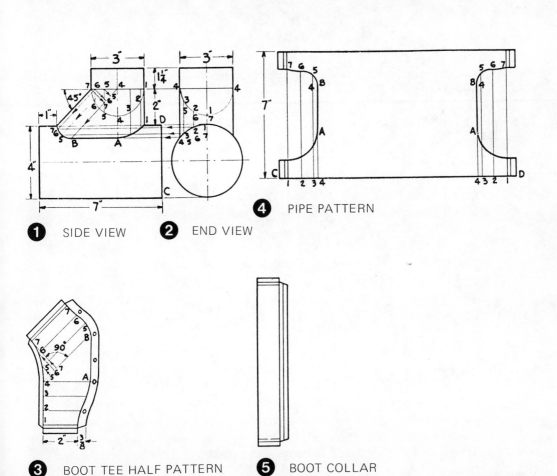

1 SIDE VIEW

2 END VIEW

4 PIPE PATTERN

3 BOOT TEE HALF PATTERN

5 BOOT COLLAR

PLATE 55   SQUARE 45-DEG. COMPOUND T

Draw the front view, Figure 1, and the end view as in Figure 2. Divide the curve 1' to 5' into equal spaces and project a line from each point to intersect the slant lines A–5 and B–5 in Figure 1.

To lay out the back pattern as in Figure 4, transfer the lengths A to 1 and B to C1 from Figure 1 to establish A–1 and B–C1' in Figure 4. Draw a line squaring from line C1'–1 at point C1' to D5'. Transfer the spaces 1' to 5' from the curve in Figure 2 to line C1'–D5' in Figure 4. Transfer the widths from line C–D to the slant lines A and B in Figure 1 to their respective lines 1' to 5' in Figure 4 obtaining the freehand curves 1' to 5 at line B and 1 to 5 at line A.

Transfer the spaces 1" to 5" from Figure 2 to lines A–A and B–B in Figures 5 and 6. Transfer the lengths from point A to points 1–5 in Figure 1 to their respective lines in Figure 5 thus obtaining the freehand curve 1 to 5.

Transfer the lengths from point B to points 1–5 in Figure 1 to their respective lines in Figure 6 thus obtaining the freehand curve 1 to 5.

To lay out the pattern as in Figure 7, transfer the lengths A to 1 and B to C1 from Figure 1 to establish A–1 and B–C1 in Figure 7.

Complete the patterns by allowing for seaming and riveting laps.

PLATE 55

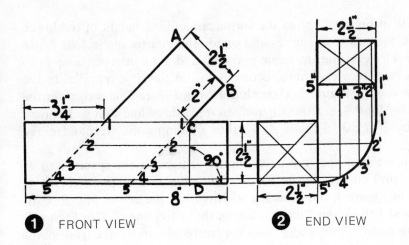

1 FRONT VIEW

2 END VIEW

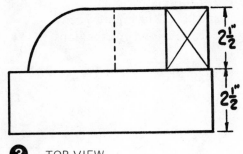

3 TOP VIEW

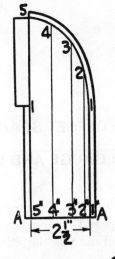

5 SIDE PATTERN

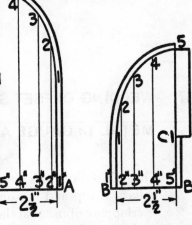

6 SIDE PATTERN

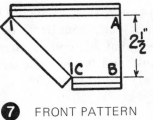

7 FRONT PATTERN

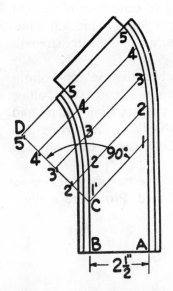

4 BACK PATTERN

PLATE 56   SLOPING HOOD ON WASTE CAN

The front view in Figure 1 shows the waste can and the height of the hood. Draw the side view as in Figure 2, and divide the quarter circle 1 to 4 into equal spaces. Draw a line up from points 2 and 3 to intersect line 1–C. Draw a slant line from each intersecting point on line 1–C parallel to the slant line 1–F toward Figure 3. Draw line 1–A in Figure 3, and transfer the heights 2–2, 3–3, and 4–C from Figure 2 to one side of line 1–A in Figure 3 represented by 2'–2", 3'–3", and A–4", thus obtaining the freehand curve 1 to 4".

To lay out the hood pattern as in Figure 4, transfer the spaces 1 to 4" from the freehand curved line in Figure 3 to each side of point B1 to 4" on line C–C in Figure 4. Transfer the widths from the center line B–C to points D, E, and F in Figure 2 to each side of the center line C–C in Figure 4, thus obtaining points D, E, and F. Draw a freehand curved line from point C to F.

Complete the pattern by allowing for a single edge and wiring edge as shown.

PLATE 57   WELDING OFFSET SEAMS, METAL 18 GAUGE AND LIGHTER

This plate illustrates the preparation for welding of center seam and the collars at top and bottom for round, or oval taper joints. This will allow overlapping of metal at the seams with a smooth surface and greater strength at the seams.

When the patterns are layed out, allow $\frac{1}{8}$ inch at the top and bottom edge of the taper joint; also allow $\frac{1}{8}$ inch at each end for center seam; allow $\frac{1}{8}$ inch at one edge of each collar. When duct continues from collars and connecting seams are welded allow $\frac{1}{8}$ inch at both edges. Use burring machine and set gauge back $\frac{5}{16}$ inch. Offset one edge of center seam on each collar and taper joint about depth of bottom roll.

Form taper joint and collars, then weld seams. Use burring machine to offset or shrink, and flange each section as illustrated. Procedure is illustrated and explained in Plate 23.

PLATE 56

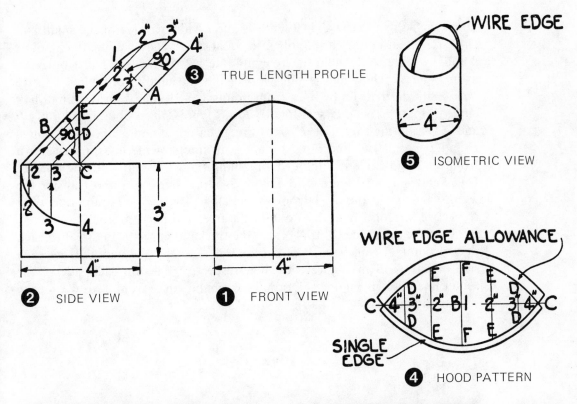

③ TRUE LENGTH PROFILE

WIRE EDGE

⑤ ISOMETRIC VIEW

② SIDE VIEW

① FRONT VIEW

WIRE EDGE ALLOWANCE

SINGLE EDGE

④ HOOD PATTERN

PLATE 57

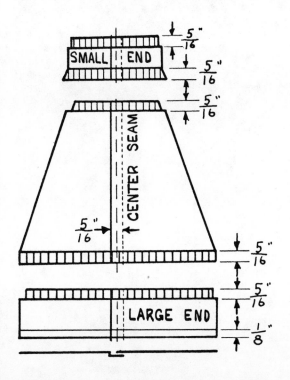

SMALL END

CENTER SEAM

LARGE END

PLATE 58   CYLINDRICAL PAN WITH EAR HANDLES

Draw the half-top view as in Figure 1, and divide one side of the small half circle representing the ear handle into equal spaces. Draw a line from points 2 and 3 to intersect the large circle and line 1–A. Draw the half-front view as in Figure 2, showing the side view of the ear handle; draw line C–F to any length desired. Draw lines from points 1, 2, 3, and 4 on the small half circle in Figure 1 to intersect line C–F in Figure 2, also obtaining points D and E. Draw the slant line F–G to the given angle and a line from points E and D parallel to line F–G, Figure 2, to intersect the lines drawn down from the large circle in Figure 1, obtaining points H and J. Draw lines C, D, E, and F from Figure 2 to Figure 3. Draw line 1–A, and transfer the widths 2–2, 3–3, and A–4 from the small half circle in Figure 1 to their respective lines in Figure 3 to obtain the freehand curve 1″ to 4″.

Transfer the spaces 1″ to 4″ from the freehand curve in Figure 3 to each side of point 1″B on line C–C in Figure 4. Transfer the widths from each side of line C–B in Figure 2 to their respective lines on each side of the center line C–C in Figure 4. Draw the freehand curve from C to C on each side as shown.

PLATE 58

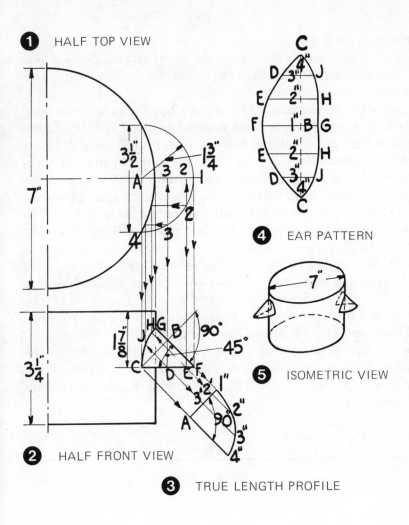

1 HALF TOP VIEW

$3\frac{1}{2}$"

$1\frac{3}{4}$"

7"

$3\frac{1}{4}$"

$1\frac{7}{8}$"

90°

45°

90°

1"

2"

3"

4"

2 HALF FRONT VIEW

3 TRUE LENGTH PROFILE

4 EAR PATTERN

C

D 4"

3"

E 2"

F 1" B G

E 2"

D 3"

J 4"

C

5 ISOMETRIC VIEW

7"

PLATE 59   SCALE SCOOP

Draw the end view as in Figure 1.

Divide the small and the large circles into equal spaces. Draw a line from points 2 and 3 to intersect the large circle, and draw a line from points 5 and 6 to intersect the center line A–4.

Draw the side view as in Figure 2. Then draw a line from the intersecting points of lines 1, 2, 3, and 4 on the large circle in Figure 1 to intersect the center line 1–B in Figure 2. Continue drawing lines 2 and 3 parallel to the slant line C–D, to intersect lines 2 and 3 drawn from the small circle, thus establishing points 2' and 3'. Draw lines 5 and 6 from Figure 1 to intersect line 1–B in Figure 2. Draw lines from points B, J, and K parallel to the slant line C–E, to Figure 3. Draw line A–4, and transfer the widths A–7, 6–6, and 5–5 from Figure 1 to their respective lines in Figure 3 to obtain the freehand curve 4″ to 7″.

The shape of the top edge of the scoop is shown in Figure 4.

Transfer the spaces 4″ to 7″ from the freehand curve in Figure 3 on true length profile to line $B7″$ in Figure 5. Transfer the widths from each side of line B–F in Figure 2 to their respective lines on each side of line $B7″$–$B7″$ in Figure 5. Draw the freehand curved lines from $B7″$ to $B7″$.

To lay out the base pattern as in Figure 6, draw line 4–4 equal to the circumference of the base, and divide it into equal spaces. Transfer the lengths of the base stem from Figure 2 to their lines in Figure 6 to obtain the freehand curve 4' to 4'.

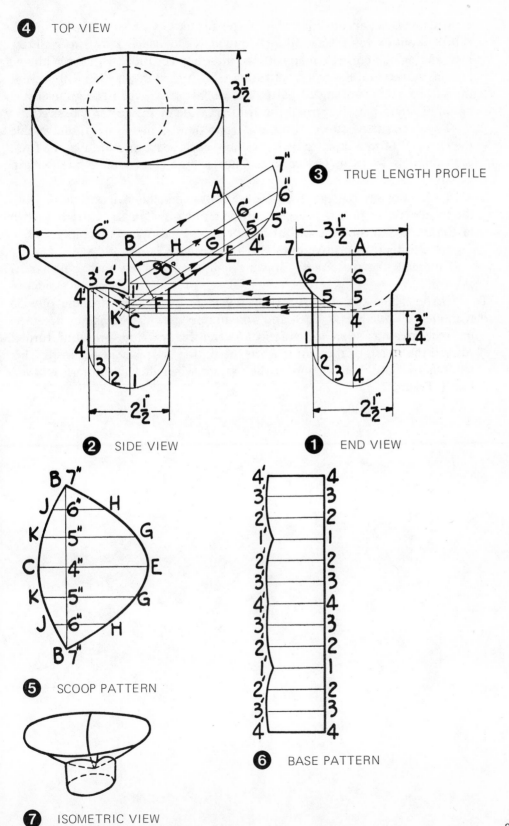

PLATE 59

4 TOP VIEW

$3\frac{1}{2}"$

3 TRUE LENGTH PROFILE

7"
6"
6"
5"

6"
6'
5'
5"
4"

$3\frac{1}{2}"$

D B H G E 7 A

90°

3' 2' J

4'

K C F

6 6
5 5
4

$\frac{3"}{4}$

4

3 2 1

1

2 3 4

$2\frac{1}{2}"$

$2\frac{1}{2}"$

2 SIDE VIEW

1 END VIEW

B 7"
J 6" H
K 5" G
C 4" E
K 5" G
J 6" H
B 7"

5 SCOOP PATTERN

4' 4
3' 3
2' 2
1' 1
2' 2
3' 3
4' 4
3' 3
2' 2
1' 1
2' 2
3' 3
4 4

6 BASE PATTERN

7 ISOMETRIC VIEW

89

PLATE 60   O-G BOX GUTTER OUTSIDE CORNER MITER

This plate shows an outside corner miter for an O-G gutter. The $\frac{3}{4}$-in. lap is turned out on top instead of turned toward the inside. This is to facilitate in soldering the corner miter without interference from this lap. With the lap turned out and the $\frac{1}{2}$-in. stiffening edge turned down, this will prevent the soiling and streaking of gutter and facial board when the gutter overflows. (The lap may be turned toward the inside of the gutter if desired.)

To lay out the pattern, draw the front view as in Figure 1, and divide the curve 5–14 into equal spaces. Number each bend, and draw a line from each point, 1 to 18 in Figure 1, to intersect the center miter line $A-B$ in Figure 2.

To lay out the pattern as in Figure 3, transfer the spaces 1 to 18 from the front view, Figure 1, to represent the stretch-out for the pattern 1 to 18 in Figure 3. Transfer the widths from line 1–18 to the center line $A-B$ in Figure 2 to their respective lines 1 to 18 in Figure 3.

Complete the pattern by drawing a line connecting each point from A to B.

NOTE: The front drip, or stiffening edge, turned toward the outside identified by numbers 1, 2, 3, and 4 in Figure 1 front view is not accepted in some areas as standard practice. Therefore, this edge must be turned toward the inside of the gutter when the profile is drawn in Figure 1. This will change only that portion of the pattern when the full pattern is layed out in Figure 2.

PLATE 60

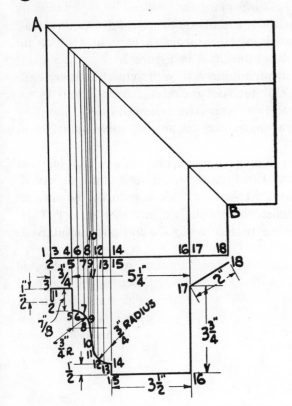

2 TOP VIEW

1 FRONT VIEW

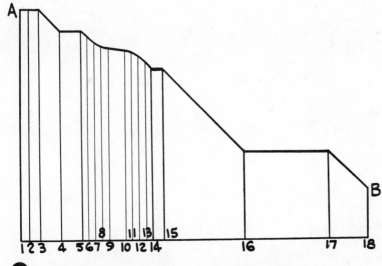

3 PATTERN

PLATE 61   O-G BOX GUTTER INSIDE CORNER MITER

This plate shows an inside corner miter for an O-G gutter. The procedure for this plate is identical to the previous plate.

Draw the front view as in Figure 1, and divide the curve 5–14 into equal spaces. Number each bend, and draw a line from each point 1 to 18 in Figure 1 to intersect the center miter line A–B in Figure 2.

Transfer the spaces 1 to 18 from Figure 1 to represent the stretch-out for the pattern 1 to 18 in Figure 3. Transfer the widths from line 1–18 to the center line A–B in Figure 2 to their respective lines in Figure 3.

Complete the pattern by drawing a line connecting each point from A to B.

NOTE: The front drip, or stiffening edge, turned toward the outside identified by numbers 1, 2, 3, and 4 in Figure 1 front view is not accepted in some areas as standard practice. Therefore, this edge must be turned toward the inside of the gutter when the profile is drawn in Figure 1. This will change only that portion of the pattern when the full pattern is layed out in Figure 2.

PLATE 61

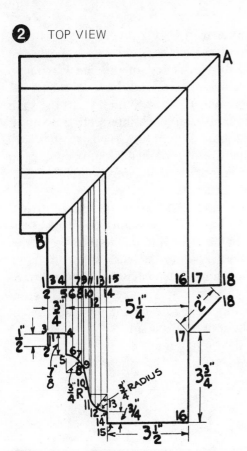

2 TOP VIEW

1 FRONT VIEW

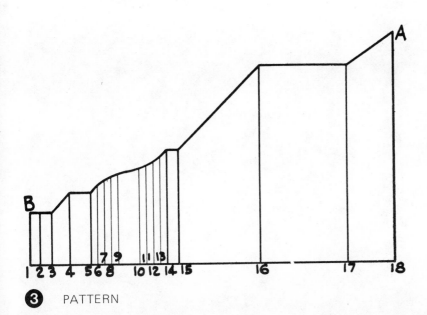

3 PATTERN

PLATE 62   A PARALLELOGRAM-SHAPED HOOD

The front view in Figure 1 and the end view in Figure 2 need not be drawn, they are shown merely to illustrate the shape of the hood.

Draw the top view as in Figure 3 and a section of the end view as in Figure 4. Divide the arc 1″ to 5″ into equal spaces, and draw a straight line through each division point to intersect line 1″–C in Figure 4 and the slant miter line 5–D in Figure 3. Draw a line up from each intersecting point on line 5–D parallel to line D–E toward Figure 5, and draw the base line C–1′. Transfer the heights from the base line C–1″ to points 2″, 3″, 4″, and 5″ in Figure 4 to their respective lines in Figure 5, establishing points 2′, 3′, 4′, and 5′. Then draw the freehand curve 1′ to 5′.

To lay out the end pattern A as in Figure 6, transfer the spaces 1′ to 5′ from the freehand curve in Figure 5 to line 1′–5′ in Figure 6. Transfer the widths from each side of line 1–5, on section A in Figure 3, to their respective lines in Figure 6, thus obtaining the freehand curve on each side.

To lay out the side pattern B as in Figure 7, transfer the spaces 1″ to 5″ on the curve in Figure 4 to line 1″–5″ in Figure 7. Transfer the widths from each side of line 1–5, on section B in Figure 3, to each side of line 1″–5″ in Figure 7, thus obtaining the freehand curve on each side.

An isometric view of the hood is shown in Figure 8.

PLATE 62

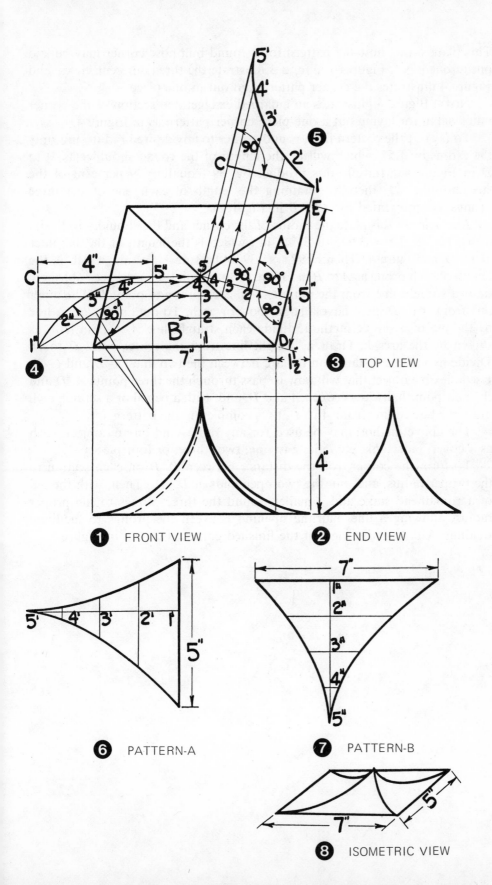

1 FRONT VIEW

2 END VIEW

3 TOP VIEW

4

5

6 PATTERN-A

7 PATTERN-B

8 ISOMETRIC VIEW

95

PLATE 63   ROUND-CORNER PATTERN

This plate shows how the pattern for a round bull nose corner may be laid out in one piece. Figures 1, 2, and 3 illustrate the three different views, and Figure 4 illustrates the corner pattern laid out in one piece.

NOTE: Figure 6 illustrates an enlarged exaggerated section of the corner miter detail for laying out a one-piece corner pattern as in Figure 4.

To lay out the pattern for a round corner to any desired radius, multiply the radius by 1.57, which will be the length of the round shoulder as D to D in Figure 4. Multiply this product by .39 (equaling 39 per cent of the stretch-out D–D) thereby obtaining the length of each one of the three prongs as represented by A to B in Figure 4.

Example: In this plate the radius of the corner and the shoulder is $2\frac{1}{2}$ in. Thus, $1.57 \times 2.5 = 3.925$ or $3\frac{15}{16}$ in., which is the length of the shoulder D to D in Figure 4. Then, $3.925 \times .39 = 1.53$ or $1\frac{17}{32}$ in., which is the length of each prong as A to B in Figure 4. Since point A has been established, draw a straight line from the point (A) on each prong to point D. The miter line from A to D must have a slight bow or arch. To obtain this miter line by the use of a simple method, divide each straight line A to D in half, as shown by the arcs E. Draw a straight line from the center point C to D. Divide in half the distance on the arc between the two lines A–D and C–D. Use a flexible object that will bow to pass through the three points A–D and the new point halfway between A and D, and, with a pencil or a scratch awl, draw the bowed line from A to D, thus completing the pattern.

The above method may be used for any radius and on any object, such as a cover, pan, tank, etc., made in one, two, three, or four pieces.

To form the corner, roll the distance between D–D on each section to the proper radius, and join the two open ends at D'–D'. Then, with the aid of a roundhead stake and a mallet, round the three prongs to the proper radius, allowing a fine, hairline opening between the prongs to facilitate welding. A perspective view of the finished corner is shown in Figure 5.

PLATE 63

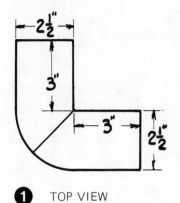

1 TOP VIEW

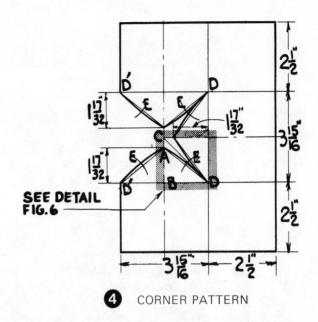

4 CORNER PATTERN

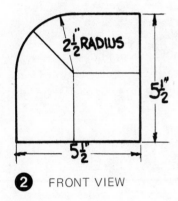

2 FRONT VIEW

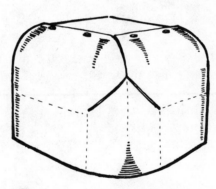

5 PERSPECTIVE VIEW

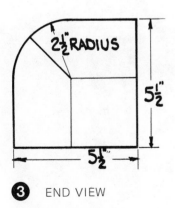

3 END VIEW

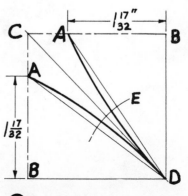

6 ENLARGED SECTION OF CORNER MITER

97

PLATE 60

PART TWO
Radial Line Development

PLATE 64   **SQUARE TAPERING JOINT IN ONE PIECE**

To lay out a tapering joint in one piece, draw the top view, or construct only the triangle *A–B–H* as in Figure 1, which represents the slant corner. To obtain a front view as in Figure 2, draw the center line *A–D* to any length desired. Draw the top and base lines to the given height, and set one half of the width of the top on each side of point *E*, and one half of the width of the base on each side of point *D*. Draw a slant line from point *G* crossing through point *F*, to intersect the center line, thus establishing point *A*. It is necessary to construct only one half of the front view as represented by *E–F* and *D–G*. Transfer the slant length *A–B* from Figure 1 to the base line *D* to *B* in Figure 2. Draw the slant line *B* to *A*, crossing line *C*. This line represents the true length of the corner on the taper pattern.

To lay out the taper pattern as in Figure 3, use the distance *A* to *B* in Figure 2 as a radius, and point *A* in Figure 3 as a center. Strike a large arc at point *B*. Set the dividers to equal the width of any side in Figure 1, and set that width four times on arc *B* to represent the sides of the pattern. Draw straight lines connecting each point *B*. Draw a line from each point *B* to point *A*. Use the distance *A* to *C* in Figure 2 as a radius, and draw the arc at point *C* in Figure 3. Draw straight lines connecting the intersecting points of arc *C* and the lines drawn from *B* to *A*.

PLATE 65   **SMOKESTACK BASE ON 30-DEG. PITCH**

To draw the front view as in Figure 2, follow the same procedure as in the previous plate. Draw a 30-deg. line at points *G* to *E*, which represents the pitch of the roof. It is not necessary to construct a full top view. The triangle *A–B–H* in Figure 1 will be sufficient. Transfer the slant length *A–B* from Figure 1 to the base line *H* to *B* in Figure 2. Draw the slant line *B* to *A*, crossing lines *C* and *D*. Use the distance *A* to *B* in Figure 2 as a radius, and point *A* in Figure 3 as a center. Draw a large arc at *B*. Set the dividers to equal the width of the base in Figure 2, and set that width four times on the base line *B* in Figure 3. Draw a line from each point *B* to point *A*. Use the distance *A* to *C* in Figure 2 as a radius and point *A* in Figure 3 as a center. Draw arc *C*. Use *A* to *D* in Figure 2 as a radius, and draw arc *D* in Figure 3. Draw slant lines from any two points represented by *B* and connect points *C*. Make seam allowances, and complete the pattern as shown.

To lay out the roof flange as in Figure 4, transfer the slant length *E–G* from Figure 2 to the center line in Figure 4. The width of the base is equal to the dimensions as shown in Figure 2. The width of the top is equal to the distance *E* to *F* in Figure 2. The $\frac{3}{4}$-in. allowance on the inside will be bent up and riveted on the inside of the stack base. The 1-in. allowance for flashing on the outside is for school practice only. This allowance is usually 6 to 8 in. on practical jobs to avoid leakage.

Lay out the stack collar as in Figure 5.

PLATE 64

1 TOP VIEW

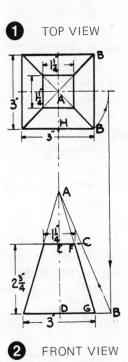

3 TAPER PATTERN

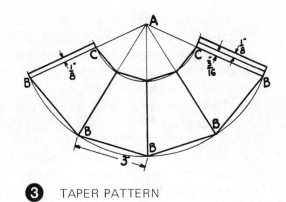

2 FRONT VIEW

PLATE 65

1 TOP VIEW

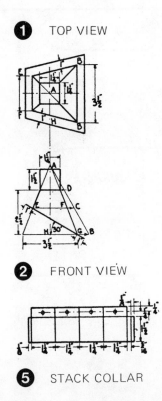

2 FRONT VIEW

5 STACK COLLAR

3 STACK BASE PATTERN

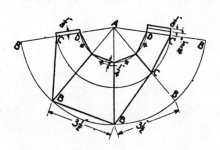

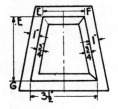

4 ROOF FLANGE

PLATE 66   SMOKESTACK BASE ON A 30-DEG. RIDGE

Construct a triangle as $A-B-E$ in the top view, Figure 1.

Draw the front view, Figure 2, using the same procedure as in the previous plates. Draw a 30-deg. line F to G, and transfer the distance $A-B$ from Figure 1 to the base line E to B in Figure 2. Draw a line from B to A, crossing lines C and D.

To lay out the stack-base pattern as in Figure 4, use the same procedure as in the previous plates. Use the distance A to C in Figure 2 as a radius, and use point A in Figure 4 as a center. Strike arc C, crossing line B. Draw a straight line from C to C, crossing the center line E. Draw a slant line from each point B to the crossing point of the straight line $C-C$ and the center line E. This represents the cutout for the 30-deg. pitch.

To lay out the roof flange as in Figure 5, transfer the slant length G to F from Figure 2 to each side of point G to F in Figure 5. Also transfer the distance G to H from Figure 2 to each side of point G to H in Figure 5. Allow for a riveting lap on the inside and for the flashing on the outside, completing the pattern as shown.

PLATE 66

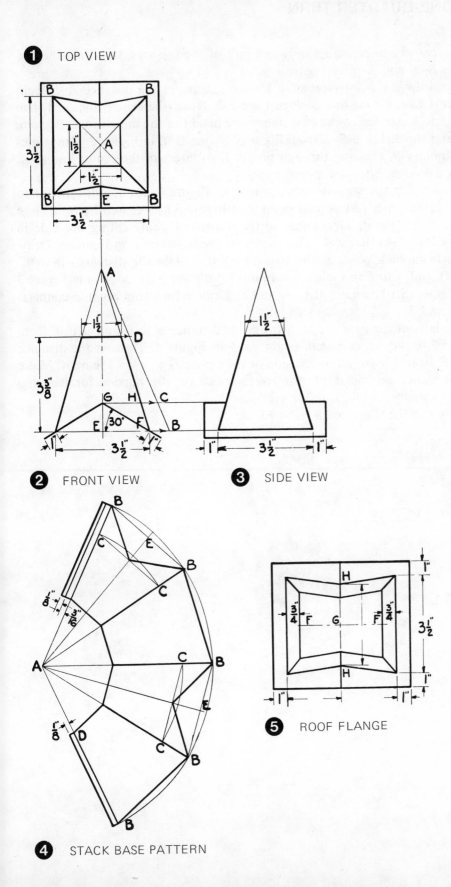

1 TOP VIEW

2 FRONT VIEW

3 SIDE VIEW

4 STACK BASE PATTERN

5 ROOF FLANGE

PLATE 67   **SMOKESTACK BASE ON 30-DEG. PITCH
AT ONE-QUARTER TURN**

It is necessary to construct only one half of the top view to obtain the distances $B-B$ and $E-E$ in Figure 1.

To draw the front view as in Figure 2, transfer the distance $B-B$ from Figure 1 to the base line $B-B$ in Figure 2. Draw the center line, and then draw line E parallel to the base line to the height of the dimensions as given. Transfer the distance $E-E$ from Figure 1 to line $E-E$ in Figure 2. Draw lines from points B, crossing through points E to intersect the center line at A. Draw a 30-deg. line from point B to F.

To lay out the stack-base pattern as in Figure 3, use the distance A to B in Figure 2 as a radius, and point A in Figure 3 as a center. Strike a large arc at B. Set the dividers equal to the dimension representing one side in Figure 1, and set that width four times on the base line B in Figure 3. Draw a line from each point at the base to point A. Use the distances A to C, A to D, and A to E in Figure 2 as radius lengths, and use point A in Figure 3 as a center. Strike an arc at C, D and E. Draw a line from point B connecting C and D.

To lay out the roof flange, transfer the distance B to G and G to F from Figure 2 to the center line $B-G$ and $G-F$ in Figure 4. Transfer the distance G to C from Figure 2 to each side of the center G to C in Figure 4. Make an allowance on the inside for riveting and on the outside for flashing. This is usually 6 to 8 in. on practical work.

Lay out the stack collar as in Figure 5.

PLATE 67

1 TOP VIEW

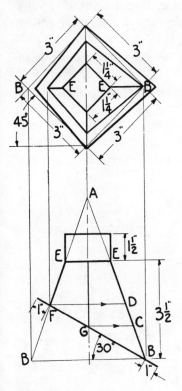

2 FRONT VIEW

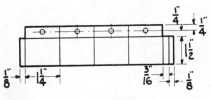

4 ROOF FLANGE PATTERN

5 STACK COLLAR

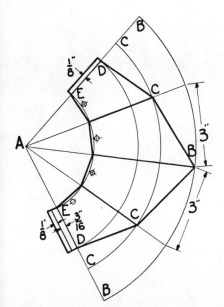

3 STACK BASE PATTERN

PLATE 68 **SMOKESTACK BASE ON 30-DEG. RIDGE
AT ONE-QUARTER TURN**

Construct the triangle $A-B-E$ in the top view, Figure 1. Transfer the distance $A-B$ from Figure 1 to each side of the center line, to obtain points $B-B$ in Figure 2. Draw the 30-deg. angle line from point B, intersecting the center line at point E.

Lay out the roof flange as in Figure 4, using the same procedure as in the previous plates.

Lay out the stack base as in Figure 3, using the same procedure as in the previous plates.

Lay out the stack collar as in Figure 5.

PLATE 68

1 TOP VIEW

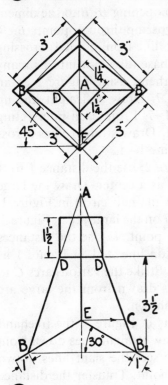

2 FRONT VIEW

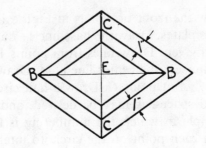

4 ROOF FLANGE PATTERN

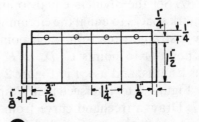

5 STACK COLLAR

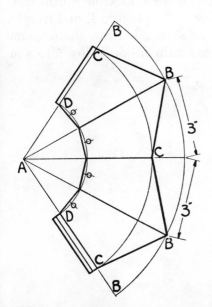

3 STACK BASE PATTERN

PLATE 69   ROUND SMOKESTACK BASE ON A 30-DEG. PITCH

Draw the front profile as in Figure 1, using the same procedure as in previous plates. Draw the base line 1–7 and the top opening B–B to the dimensions given. Draw lines from points 1 and 7, crossing through points B–B, to intersect the center line at A. Draw a 30-deg. line from point 1, crossing line 7–A at point C. Draw a half circle at the base, divide it into as many equal spaces as may be desired, and number them, using Figure 1 as an example in which the numbering is from 1 to 7. Draw a straight line up from each point on the circle to intersect line 1–7. From each intersecting point on line 1–7, continue the lines to point A. Draw straight lines across from points C, D, E, F, G, and H to intersect line 1–A.

To lay out the stack-base pattern as in Figure 2, use the distance 1 to A in Figure 1 as a radius and point A in Figure 2 as a center. Draw the large arc 7–7. Set the dividers equal to any space on the half circle in Figure 1, and mark spaces to equal the circumference 1 to 7 on the large arc in Figure 2. Draw a straight line from each point 1 to 7 to point A. Use the distances from point A to points C, D, E, F, G, and H on line A–1 in Figure 1 as radius lengths, and use A in Figure 2 as a center. Strike the various arcs C to H in Figure 2 to intersect their respective lines drawn from the large arc 1 to 7. Draw a freehand curve from 1 to C as shown.

To lay out the opening for the roof flange as in Figure 3, the freehand curve 1 to C in Figure 1 must be developed. Draw straight lines down from points C, D, E, G, and H on line 1–C to intersect the slant lines drawn from points 2, 3, 5, and 6 to the center radius point. Transfer the distance F–F from the upper portion of the profile to obtain the distance from the radius point to point F on line 4. Draw a freehand curve, crossing through the intersecting points from 1 to C. Transfer the spaces 1 to C from the slant line in Figure 1 to the center line 1 to C in Figure 3. Pick the widths from points D, E, F, G, and H to the center line 1–7 in Figure 1, and transfer them to each side of the center line 1–C in Figure 3. Draw the freehand curve 1 to C and allow for a riveting flange on the inside. Allow 6 to 8 in. for a flashing on the outside edge.

Lay out the stack collar as in Figure 4.

PLATE 69

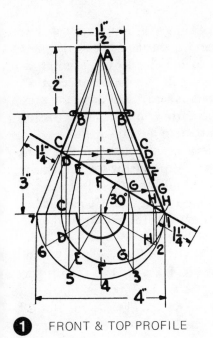

① FRONT & TOP PROFILE

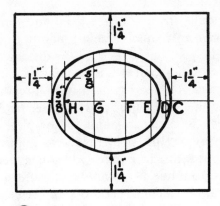

③ ROOF FLANGE

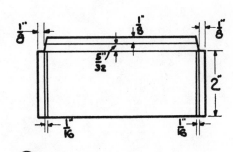

④ STACK COLLAR

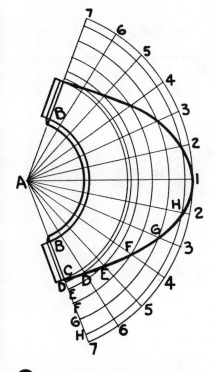

② STACK BASE PATTERN

PLATE 70   **ROUND SMOKESTACK BASE ON THE RIDGE**

OF A ROOF AT 30 DEG.

Draw only one half of the front and top profile as shown in Figure 1. Use the same procedure to obtain points C, D, and E on the slant 30-deg. line as in the previous plate. Use the distances A to B and A to 1 in Figure 1 as radius lengths to draw the arcs B and 1 in Figure 2. Use the distances A–C, A–D, and A–E on line A–1 in Figure 1 as radius lengths to draw the arcs, C, D, and E in Figure 2. Draw a freehand curve from points 1 to 4, crossing through the arcs C, D, and E. Complete the pattern as shown.

To lay out the roof flange as in Figure 3, transfer the spaces C to 1 from the 30-deg. line in Figure 1, to the center line C to 1 in Figure 3. Pick the widths from line 1 to points C, D, and E in the half-top profile in Figure 1, and transfer them to each side of the center line 1–1 at points C, D, and E in Figure 3. Make the necessary allowances to complete the pattern as shown.

Lay out the stack collar as in Figure 4.

PLATE 70

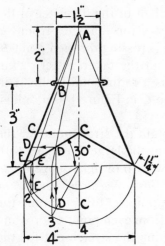

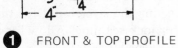

1 FRONT & TOP PROFILE

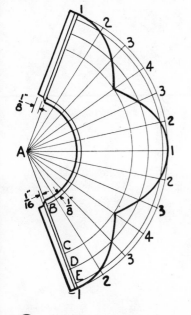

2 STACK BASE PATTERN

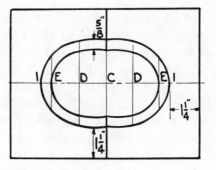

3 ROOF FLANGE

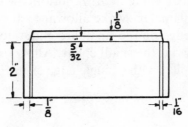

4 STACK COLLAR

PLATE 71   ROUND EQUAL-TAPER JOINT

To draw the front profile as in Figure 1, set one half of the diameter of the base from the center line to *C*, and one half of the top diameter from the center line to *B*. Draw the slant line from point *C*, crossing through point *B*, to intersect the center line at point *A*. To lay out the taper pattern as in Figure 2, use the distance *A* to *B* in Figure 1 as a radius, and point *A* in Figure 2 as a center to strike arc *B*. Then use *A* to *C* in Figure 1 as a radius, and *A* in Figure 2 as a center to strike arc *C*.

A more accurate method may be used to obtain the stretch-out for the taper pattern by finding the true circumference of the large diameter, with the aid of a flexible ruler, a tape line, or a narrow strip of light-gauge metal equal to the circumference. Set *one of the above three measuring devices, or implements that may be used*, along the arc from point *C* to *C* to equal the circumference of the large diameter. Draw a line from each point *C*, crossing the throat curve at *B–B*, automatically establishing the stretch-out for the small diameter. Make allowance at each end for lock seaming. Allow for a single edge on the small arc and a double edge on the large arc.

Lay out the small collar. Allow for a double edge as in Figure 3, and the large collar with a single edge as in Figure 4. Notch all patterns as shown.

PLATE 71

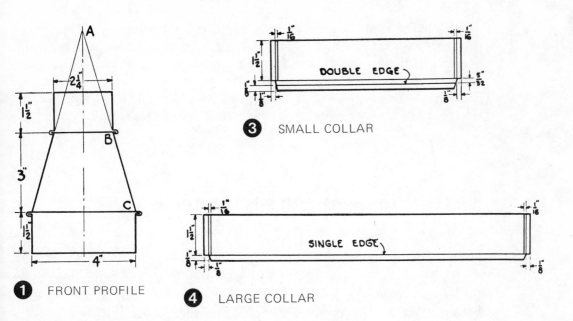

① FRONT PROFILE

③ SMALL COLLAR

④ LARGE COLLAR

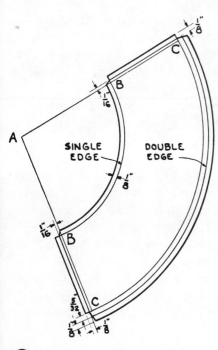

② TAPER PATTERN

PLATE 72   ROUND EQUAL-TAPER JOINT

This plate illustrates that only a half-front profile is necessary to develop a full taper pattern, as shown in Figure 1. Draw *B–D* and *C–E* equal to only one half of the full diameters shown in the top view, Figure 2. The arcs *B* and *C* are drawn over the profile, and that portion of the metal will then be included in the pattern without any waste for profile drawing. This is considered a quick method for laying out a short equal-tapered fitting.

PLATE 73   SMALL- AND LARGE-END PIPE PATTERNS

To lay out the pattern for a joint of pipe with a small end and a large end, the pattern will be tapered at the ends and curved slightly at the top and bottom. This depends on the thickness of the metal.

Figure 1 shows a pattern laid out with a small end and a large end made of $\frac{1}{4}$-in. metal. The distance *A* to *B*, which represents the small end, is equal to the given diameter. The distance *C* to *D*, which represents the large end, is equal to the given diameter plus $\frac{1}{3}$ of 7 times the thickness of the metal $(20 + \frac{1}{3} \times 7 \times .25 = 20.58)$. If the pattern is laid out in the manner shown in Figure 1, this will allow the small end to be inserted inside of the large end of the next joint far enough to make a riveting connection.

To lay out the pattern as in Figure 1, use the above method to draw the large end *C–D* and the small end *A–B*. To complete the pattern, use point *A* as a center and *A* to *C* as a radius to draw an arc from *C* to *E*. Keep the dividers set, and use point *B* as a center to draw an arc from *D* to *F*. Use *C* as a center to draw an arc from *A* to *G*. Use *D* as a center to draw an arc from *B* to *H*. Use the distance *A* to *B* (the small end) as a radius, with *A* as a center, to draw an arc crossing the large arc at *H*. Use *B* as a center to draw an arc at *G*. Use the distance *C* to *D* (the large end) as a radius, with *D* as a center, to draw an arc at *E*. Use *C* as a center to draw an arc at *F*. Use any object that may be flexible enough (such as a ruler or a strip of light metal) to be held at the ends and pulled to form a light arch. Place this arch so that it will rest on points *H*, *A*, *B*, and *G*. Use a pencil or a scratch awl to draw the arc at the top. Repeat the above procedure to draw an arc crossing points *E*, *D*, *C*, and *F*. Draw a straight line from *F* to *G* and *H* to *E*.

The circumference is equal to the diameter times 3.1416. The distance *H* to *G*, however, is equal to only three times the diameter. We must, therefore, multiply the diameter by .1416 $(20 \times .1416 = 2.832 \div 2 = 1.41)$ and add one half of the product to each side of the small end at points *G* and *H*. The same procedure must be repeated for the large end by multiplying the large diameter by .1416 $(20.58 \times .1416 = 2.914 \div 2 = 1.45$ in.) and adding one half of the product to each side of the large end at points *E* and *F*.

The inside diameter of both ends will be the thickness of the metal less than the dimension shown when rolled into a cylinder.

PLATE 72

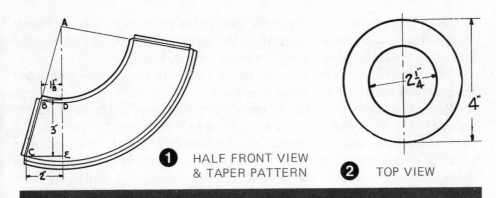

① **HALF FRONT VIEW & TAPER PATTERN**

② **TOP VIEW**

PLATE 73

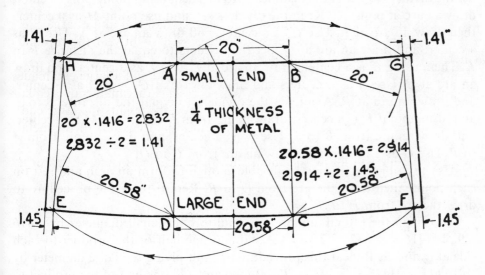

PLATE 74   PATTERN FOR TAPER JOINT

To lay out the pattern as in Figure 1, observe the enlarged exaggerated taper of two spaces in Figure 2, illustrating the procedure for obtaining points J and K on the pattern layout for the taper joint in Figure 1.

NOTE: This procedure may only be used on long taper joints with slight variations in the small and large diameters.

Draw line C–D or small diameter, and line A–B or large diameter. Draw a line from D to G and another from B to F so that each is on a 90-deg. angle to the slant line D–B. Divide the distance G–H in half, thus obtaining point J. Divide the distance E–F in half, thus obtaining point K. Set the divider to equal the distance D to K. Using point D as a center, draw an arc from points K to L. Keep the dividers set for all the remaining lengths. Using point B as a center, draw an arc from J to M. Using A as a center, draw an arc from J to N. Using C as a center, draw an arc from K to O. Set the dividers to equal the distance D to J. Then, using point D as a center, draw an arc at point M. Keep the dividers set, and use point M as a center; then draw an arc at R. Use C as a center, and draw an arc at N. Use N as a center, and draw an arc at Q. Set the dividers to equal the distance B to K. Then, using B as a center, draw an arc at L. Use L as a center, and draw an arc at S. Use A as a center, and draw an arc at O. Use O as a center, and draw an arc at P. Again set the dividers to equal the distance B to J, and, using point L as a center, draw an arc from D to R. Use M as a center, and draw an arc from B to S. Use N as a center, and draw an arc from A to P. Use O as a center, and draw an arc from C to Q.

Use any object that may be flexible enough to form an arch and rest on each point; then draw the arc from Q to R. Repeat the same procedure to draw the arc from P to S.

To obtain the full circumferences, multiply the small diameter by .1416 ($29 \times .1416 = 2.832 \div 2 = 1.41$) and add one half of the product to each side at Q and R. Repeat this procedure by multiplying the large diameter by .1416 ($24 \times .1416 = 3.398 \div 2 = 1.699$) and add one half of the product to each side at P and S. This will allow the inside diameter of both ends to be the thickness of the metal less than the dimensions shown.

PLATE 74

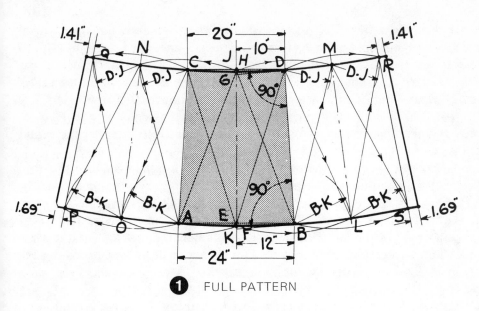

① FULL PATTERN

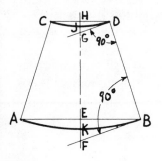

② ENLARGED EXAGGERATED
TAPER OF TWO SPACES
FOR TAPER JOINT

PLATE 75   FUNNEL

To lay out the patterns for a funnel it is necessary to draw only one half of the front profile in Figure 1. Draw the center line; then draw lines *A–B* and *D* representing the height of the funnel and spout. Mark half of the top diameter from the center line to *A*, half of the diameter from the center line at *B*, and half the diameter from the center line at *D*. Draw a slant line from *A*, crossing through point *B*, intersecting the center line at *C*. Also draw a slant line from *B*, crossing through point *D*, to intersect the center line at *E*.

To lay out the funnel pattern as in Figure 2, use the distance *C* to *B* in Figure 1 as a radius, and *C* in Figure 2 as a center. Strike arc *B*. Use the distance *C* to *A* in Figure 1 as a radius, and use *C* in Figure 2 as a center. Strike the large arc *A*. Use a flexible ruler, and set the distance equal to the circumference of the large diameter along the arc from *A* to *A* in the same procedure as in the previous plate. Draw lines from *A* to *C*, crossing the arc at *B–B*, which represents the spout opening. Make allowances for seaming and a double edge for peening.

Lay out the spout pattern as in Figure 3, using the same procedure as for the funnel pattern. Use the distances *E* to *D* and *E* to *B* in Figure 1 as radius lengths to draw the arcs *D* and *B* in Figure 3. Set the distance equal to the circumference of the large end of the spout along the arc *B* to *B*. Draw lines from each point *B* to point *E*, and make allowances for soldering laps on one side and on the top arc.

Lay out the rim pattern as in Figure 4 to equal the full circumference. Make an allowance for a wiring edge and a single edge for peening. Allow for a lock seam, and notch it as shown.

PLATE 75

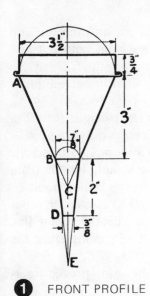

1 FRONT PROFILE

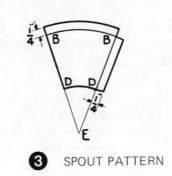

3 SPOUT PATTERN

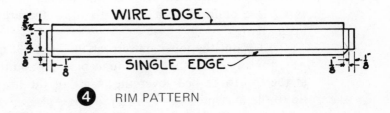

WIRE EDGE

SINGLE EDGE

4 RIM PATTERN

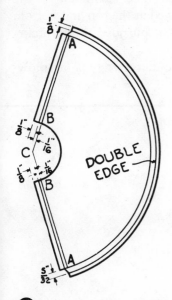

DOUBLE EDGE

2 FUNNEL PATTERN

PLATE 76   PINT MEASURE

To obtain the side profile as in Figure 1, draw the height and the top and bottom diameters to the given dimensions. Draw lines from points E and F through points 1 and 9, to intersect the center line at point A. Draw the half circle 1 to 9 at the top to establish point B. Draw slant lines from point B, crossing through points 1 and 9 to establish points C and D.

To lay out the lip pattern as in Figure 2, use the slant length B to 9 in Figure 1 as a radius. Use point B in Figure 2 as a center, draw the circle, and transfer the spaces 1 to 9 from the half circle in Figure 1 to the circle drawn 9 to 1 in Figure 2. Transfer the distances 9 to C and 1 to D from Figure 1 to lines 9–C and 1–D in Figure 2. To obtain the radius point G, bisect line C–D, by drawing an arc from points C and D to cross each other at L and M, and then draw a line through L–M crossing the center line B–C. Use point G as a center to draw the arc D–C–D, completing the lip pattern.

To lay out the taper pattern as in Figure 3, use the same procedure as used for any equal-tapering round pipe. In addition, however, allow $\frac{1}{8}$ in. at the top to be bent over the inside of the lip to facilitate soldering the lip to the measure.

Lay out the handle as in Figure 4. The length D to J is equal to the distance D to J in Figure 1. A soldering lap is allowed at the top and bottom and a double hem edge is allowed on each side for the purpose of reinforcing the handle.

The bottom pattern in Figure 5 is equal to the diameter plus an allowance to be turned up for a soldering lap.

Figure 6 shows an isometric view.

PLATE 76

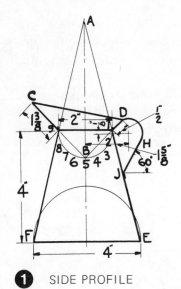

1 SIDE PROFILE

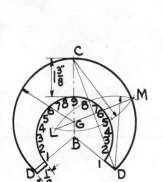

2 LIP PATTERN

3 TAPER PATTERN

4 HANDLE PATTERN

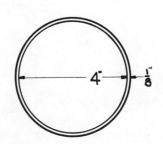

5 BOTTOM PATTERN

6 ISOMETRIC VIEW

PLATE 77   CONICAL-CAP CUTOUT

To obtain the cutout or the circumference for a conical-cap pattern, draw the front view as in Figure 1. Use A to C as a radius to draw the full circle in Figure 2 and the half circle in Figure 3. Use point C as a center to draw the arc from D to B.

The cutout on the circle in Figure 2 (the full pattern) is equal to 6.28 (or $6\frac{1}{4}$ will be accurate enough) times the distance A to B in Figure 1.

The cutout on the half circle in Figure 3 (the half pattern) is equal to 3.14 (or $3\frac{1}{8}$) times A to B in Figure 1.

Allowances for seaming may be made as desired.

PLATE 77

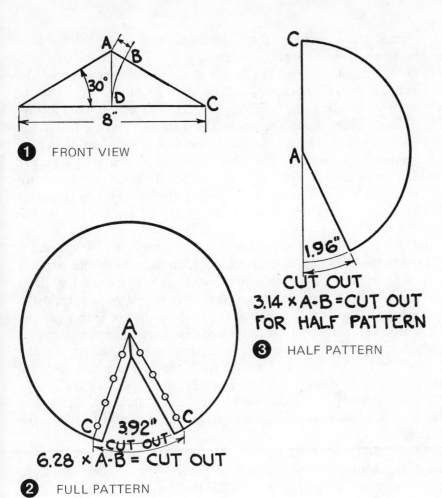

1 FRONT VIEW

2 FULL PATTERN

6.28 × A-B = CUT OUT

3.92"
CUT OUT

CUT OUT
3.14 × A-B = CUT OUT
FOR HALF PATTERN

3 HALF PATTERN

1.96"

PLATE 78   DISCHARGE-STACK HOOD

A hood, or cap, over a discharge stack should have an inside splitter cone equal to the diameter of the stack to deflect the air. Four to six band-iron brackets may be used to support the hood, depending on the size and the gauge of metal. Three or four brackets will support a medium-diameter stack.

Draw the front profile as in Figure 2. The diameter of the hood always should be twice the diameter of the stack. The distance from the top of the stack line *G–G* to the bottom of the hood line *B–B* should be one half of the stack diameter. The pitch of the hood always is 30 deg. The diameter of the inside splitter cone is equal to the diameter of the stack, and the tip of this cone begins at the base of the hood line *B–B* on the center line at point *E*. The band-iron brackets are on a 90-deg. angle from line *A–B* to the stack at point *G*.

Lay out one half of the hood pattern as in Figure 3. Use the distance *A–B* in Figure 2 as a radius to draw the arc *B* in Figure 3. The distance *B–B* is equal to one half of the circumference of the 8-in. diameter circle in Figure 1. Use the same procedure as in the previous plates to set out the distance. Use *A* to *D* in Figure 2 as a radius to draw the arc *D* in Figure 3. Divide this arc from points 1 to 4 into three equal spaces. Punch holes in every second space, such as 1 and 3, for fastening the brackets. To the distance *A–C* in Figure 2, add twice the thickness of the metal, and use this sum as a radius to draw arc *C* in Figure 3. Draw a second arc to represent the riveting line $\frac{1}{4}$ in. from arc *C*. Divide this arc from 1 to 6 into five equal spaces, and use every second space for rivet holes to fasten the splitter cone.

Lay out the inside splitter cone as in Figure 4. Use the distance *E* to *C* in Figure 2 as a radius, and use point *E* in Figure 4 as a center. Draw arc *C*. The distance *C–C* is equal to one half of the circumference of the 4-in. circle in Figure 1. Draw a second arc $\frac{1}{4}$ in. from *C*, and divide this arc into five equal spaces. Punch every second space for riveting holes. Make the necessary allowances for riveting laps to complete the pattern as shown.

Lay out the bracket pattern as in Figure 5. The distance *F–G* is equal to the distance *F–G* in Figure 2.

Lay out the stack pattern as in Figure 6 to equal the circumference of the 4-in. diameter stack in Figure 2. Draw two more lines the same distance apart as the holes shown in the bracket in Figure 5. Divide the distance on each side of the center line 1 to 7 into six equal spaces. At every second space draw a straight line up, crossing the two lines drawn parallel to the base line. Punch holes at the intersecting points to fasten the six hood brackets.

PLATE 78

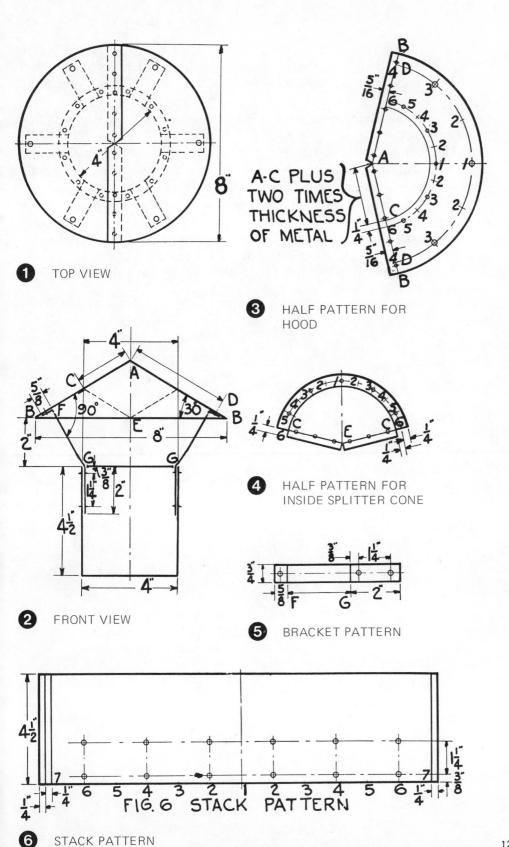

1 TOP VIEW

3 HALF PATTERN FOR HOOD

A-C PLUS TWO TIMES THICKNESS OF METAL

2 FRONT VIEW

4 HALF PATTERN FOR INSIDE SPLITTER CONE

5 BRACKET PATTERN

FIG. 6 STACK PATTERN

6 STACK PATTERN

125

PLATE 79   VENTILATOR WITH WEATHER BAND

Draw the front view as in Figure 1 to obtain the radius lengths to lay out the half-cap pattern as in Figure 3, and the collar pattern in Figure 4.

The diameter of the cap is equal to 1.40 times the diameter of the base pipe.

The remaining sections of the ventilator are equal to the proportion of the diameter as shown.

The half weather band in Figure 5 may be made in one piece with a hem-edge allowance on top. After the band has been seamed, a bead is turned out near the top and bottom edges for reinforcing.

The half-pipe pattern in Figure 6 may be laid out in one piece equal to the full circumference.

The band-iron braces, as in Figure 7, may be made of a size and weight of band iron to suit the diameter of the ventilator.

All holes should be laid out and punched in the flat pattern before forming, to facilitate the assembling of the patterns.

PLATE 79

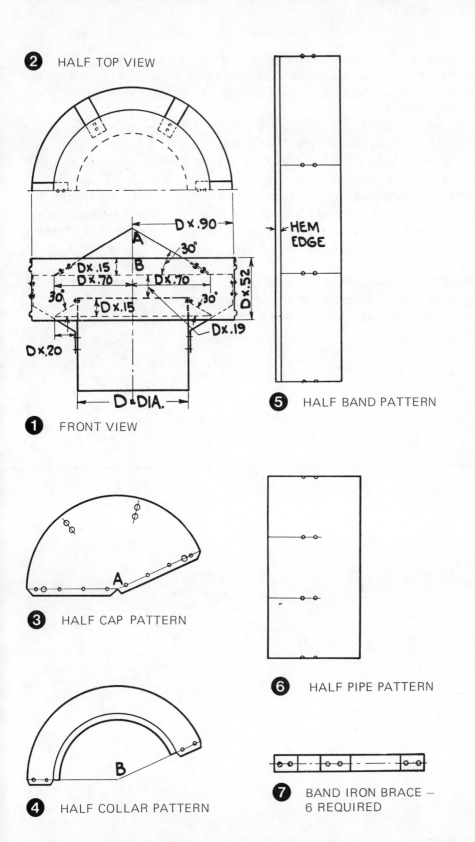

2 HALF TOP VIEW

1 FRONT VIEW

5 HALF BAND PATTERN

3 HALF CAP PATTERN

6 HALF PIPE PATTERN

4 HALF COLLAR PATTERN

7 BAND IRON BRACE —
6 REQUIRED

PLATE 80   SQUARE TAPERING T INTERSECTING CYLINDER

OFF CENTER

To obtain the front view as in Figure 1, draw line C–B, with point C off center to the dimensions, as shown. Draw a line from point B, striking the round pipe on a tangent, thus establishing point A. Draw line A–C to establish point D.

To lay out the T pattern as in Figure 3, draw line B–B to equal the dimensions as shown in Figure 2. The distance A to B is equal to the distance A–B in Figure 1. Use A to C in Figure 1 as a radius. Then, using point A in Figure 3 as a center, strike an arc at C. Use B to C in Figure 1 as a radius. Then, using point B in Figure 3 as a center, strike an arc crossing the arc at C. Draw a straight line from A to C. Transfer the distance C–D from Figure 1 to C–D in Figure 3. Using the distance O to A in Figure 1 as a radius, and points A and D in Figure 3 as centers, strike arcs to cross each other at point O. Use point O as a center, and draw the arc from A to D. Draw lines squaring from line A–C at points C and D. Mark the lengths of lines C–C and D–D to the dimensions as shown.

Complete the pattern by allowing for seaming and flanging.

PLATE 80

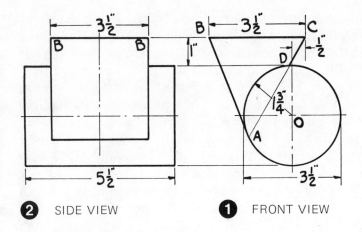

② SIDE VIEW   **①** FRONT VIEW

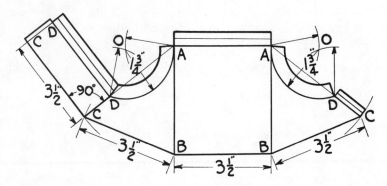

③ TEE PATTERN

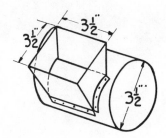

④ ISOMETRIC VIEW

PLATE 81 **SQUARE EQUAL-TAPERING T INTERSECTING A CYLINDER ON CENTER**

Draw the front view as in Figure 1. It is necessary to draw only one quarter of the top view to form the triangle to obtain the slant length $C-D$. Transfer the length $C-D$ from the top view to obtain $C-D$ in the front view. Divide one half of the top width 1 to 4 into equal spaces, and draw a line from each division point to point A. At the intersection of the circle, draw a line from each point 1 to 4 to intersect line $A-D$, which represents the true length of the corner line on the T pattern.

To lay out the T pattern as in Figure 3, use the distance $A-D$ in Figure 1 as a radius to draw the large arc in Figure 3. Mark the width of the four sides $D-D$ on the arc, and transfer the division spaces 1 to 4 from Figure 1 to lines $D-D$ in Figure 3. Draw a line from each division point 1, 2, 3, and 4 to point A. Transfer the spaces A to 1, 2, 3, and 4 on line $A-D$ in Figure 1, to lines $A-D$ in Figure 3, spaces 1, 2, 3, and 4. Draw a line across from each point, 2 to 4, crossing the lines drawn down from points 2, 3, and 4, on line $D-D$. Draw a freehand curve through the intersecting points 1 to 4 and 4 to 1.

Complete the pattern by allowing for seaming and flanging.

PLATE 81

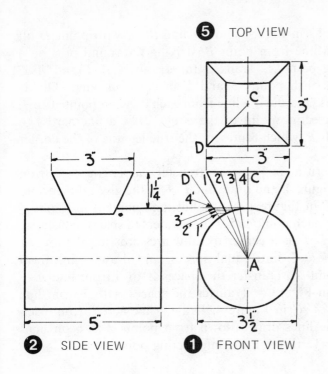

5 TOP VIEW

2 SIDE VIEW

1 FRONT VIEW

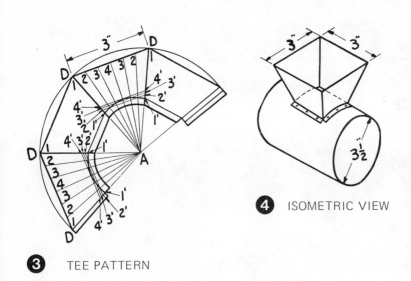

3 TEE PATTERN

4 ISOMETRIC VIEW

PLATE 82   SQUARE TAPERING T INTERSECTING CYLINDER

OFF CENTER

To obtain the front view as in Figure 1, draw line $B-D$, with point D off center, as shown. Draw a line from point B, striking the round pipe on a tangent, thus establishing point A. Transfer the distances $A-F$ and $A-C$ from the top view to establish points F and C in the front view. Divide line $B-D$ into equal spaces, and draw a line from each division point, 1 to 7, to point A. At each intersecting point of the circle, draw a line across to intersect lines $A-C$ and $A-F$, which represent the true lengths of the corner lines on the T pattern.

To lay out the T pattern as in Figure 4, transfer the length $A-B$ from Figure 1, to line $A-B$ in Figure 4, and draw line $F-F$ to the given dimension. Using the distance A to C in Figure 1 as a radius, and point A in Figure 4 as a center, strike an arc at each point C. Set the dividers to span the distance $F-F$, and use each point $F-F$ as a center to draw arcs crossing the arcs at points $C-C$. Divide lines $F-C$ into equal spaces, and draw a line from each division point to point A. Transfer the spaces A to 6 from line $A-F$ in Figure 1 to line $A-F$ in Figure 4. Transfer the spaces A to 7 from line $A-C$ in Figure 1 to lines $A-C$ in Figure 4. Draw a line across from each point, 2 to 6, crossing the lines drawn down from points 2 to 6 on lines $F-C$. Draw a freehand curve through the intersecting points A to 7.

PLATE 82

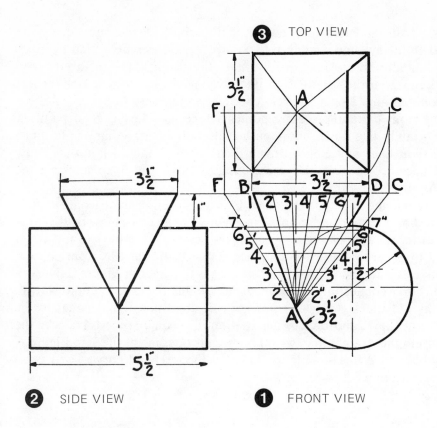

3 TOP VIEW

2 SIDE VIEW

1 FRONT VIEW

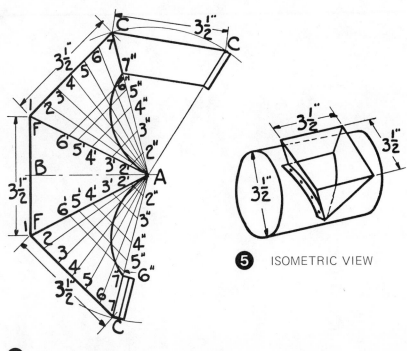

4 TEE PATTERN

5 ISOMETRIC VIEW

PLATE 83   **SQUARE T INTERSECTING A CONE**

VERTICALLY THROUGH CENTER

Draw the front and half-top view as in Figure 1. Divide one side of the square T in the half-top view into two more spaces, as represented by numbers 1, 2, and 3. Draw lines from point *B*, crossing through the division points 2 and 3 on the square T to intersect the circle. Draw a straight line from points 2 and 3 on the circle to intersect the base line 1–*B*. Draw a slant line from these intersecting points on the base line 1–*B* to point *A*. Draw a straight line down, representing one side of the square T, to intersect the slant lines 1, 2, and 3 drawn from the base line to point *A*. Draw straight lines across from the intersecting points 2 and 3, to intersect the slant line *A*–1.

To lay out the cone pattern as in Figure 2, use the slant length *A* to 1 in Figure 1 as a radius, and point *A* in Figure 2 as a center to draw the large arc. Transfer the spaces 1 to 3 from the half circle in Figure 1 to the arc in Figure 2 to equal the full circumference. Transfer the lengths from point *A* to points 1, 2, and 3 in Figure 1 to their respective lines in Figure 2. Draw a freehand curve connecting each point, thus completing the pattern as shown.

To lay out the T pattern as in Figure 3, draw line 1 to 1 equal to the perimeter of the T, and divide each section into equal spaces. Transfer the heights from the straight line, which represents one side of the T in Figure 1, to their respective lines in Figure 3. Draw the freehand curves, and complete the pattern as shown.

An isometric view is shown in Figure 4.

PLATE 83

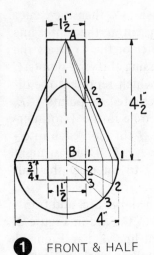

1 FRONT & HALF TOP VIEW

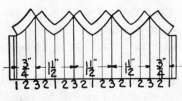

3 SQUARE PIPE PATTERN

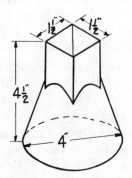

4 ISOMETRIC VIEW

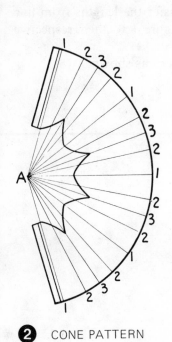

2 CONE PATTERN

PLATE 84   ROUND T INTERSECTING A CONE

FORMING A 90-DEG. ELBOW

To obtain the front view as in Figure 1, draw the base 1–7, then the center line $A–B$ to any height desired. Draw line $C–4$, representing the center line of the T. The distance C to D is equal to the diameter of the T. Draw the two slant lines from the base at points 1 and 7, crossing through points C and D, intersecting at point A. Draw lines 1 and 7, which represent the diameter of the T, to intersect the slant lines 1–7 represented by points 1–E. Draw lines through the division points on the half circle in the T to intersect the slant line 1–E. Draw slant lines from point A through each intersecting point on line 1–E, to intersect the base line 1–7. Draw straight lines down from the intersecting points on line 1–7 to intersect the half circle.

To lay out the cone pattern as in Figure 2, draw the large arc, and transfer the spaces 1 to 7 from the half circle in Figure 1 to the arc in Figure 2. Transfer the lengths from point A to 7–1 on the slant line A–1 in Figure 1 to their respective lines in Figure 2. Draw the freehand curve 1 to 1, completing the pattern as shown.

To lay out the T pattern as in Figure 3, draw line 1–1 to equal the circumference, and divide it into equal spaces. Transfer the lengths from line 1–7 on the T profile to the slant line 1–E in Figure 1 to their respective lines in Figure 3.

Draw the freehand curve, completing the pattern as shown.

An isometric view is shown in Figure 4.

PLATE 84

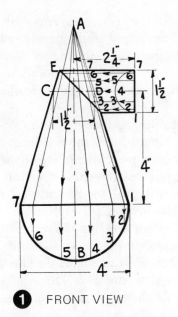

1 FRONT VIEW

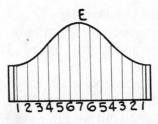

3 MITERED PIPE PATTERN

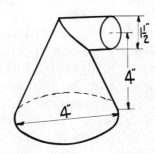

4 ISOMETRIC VIEW

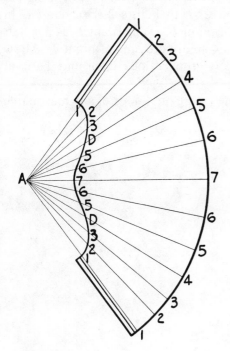

2 CONE PATTERN

PLATE 85   RECTANGULAR HOOD

To lay out the hood patterns as in Figures 3 and 4, it is necessary to draw only a right angle as $A–D$ in Figure 1 to equal the height of the hood, and a base line to any length desired. The triangle then is completed as $A–B$ and C in Figure 2.

Transfer the lengths $A–B$ and $A–C$ from the triangle in Figure 2 to the base line in Figure 1.

To lay out the full pattern as in Figure 3, use the slant length D to C in Figure 1 as a radius to draw the large circle in Figure 3. Set the dividers to equal the length of the hood $C–C$ in Figure 2; then place one point of the dividers on the circle, and swing the other leg to cross the circle, thus obtaining the length of the hood $C–C$ in Figure 3. Repeat the procedure by spanning the dividers equal to the width of the hood $C–E$ in Figure 2. Using points $C–C$ in Figure 3 as centers, strike arcs crossing the circle at $E–E$. Using $D–B$ in Figure 1 as a radius and point D in Figure 3 as a center, strike the small arc at B. Set the dividers equal to $E–B$ in Figure 2. Then, using points E in Figure 3 as centers, strike arcs at points $B–B$. Draw lines connecting all points, completing the pattern as shown. A riveting seam may be used if desired.

To lay out a half pattern as in Figure 4, draw line $C–C$ to equal the length of the hood. Line $D–B$ is equal to the slant length $D–B$ in Figure 1. Set the dividers equal to the width of the hood $C–E$ in Figure 2. Use point C in Figure 4 as a center, and strike an arc at point E. Using point D as a center and D to C in Figure 4 as a radius, draw an arc crossing at point E. Allow laps, and lay out rivet holes as shown. A grooved lock seam may be used if desired.

The method in Figure 4 is preferred in laying out hoods of any reasonable size.

PLATE 85

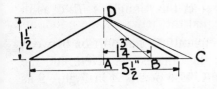

1 FRONT VIEW

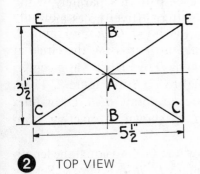

2 TOP VIEW

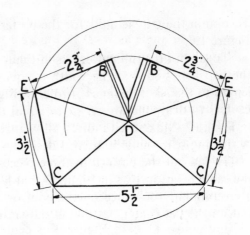

3 FULL PATTERN

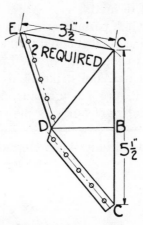

4 HALF PATTERN

PLATE 86   OBLONG HOOD OR COVER

To obtain the true lengths for the patterns, erect the triangle $A-B-C$ as in Figure 1.

To lay out the full pattern as in Figure 3, lay out the flat portion between the two cones so that the width is equal to the dimensions given, and the length to the slant distance A to B in Figure 1. Use points A in Figure 3 as centers to draw the arcs $B-B$ to equal the length of the half circle B to B in Figure 2. Make the required allowance to complete the pattern as shown. A riveting seam may be used if desired.

To lay out the pattern in three pieces as shown in Figures 4 and 5, use the same procedure as in Figure 3, but lay out each pattern separately, with a riveting-lap allowance on the end, or cone, pattern. Rivet holes are laid out on the flat center pattern as shown in Figure 5.

PLATE 86

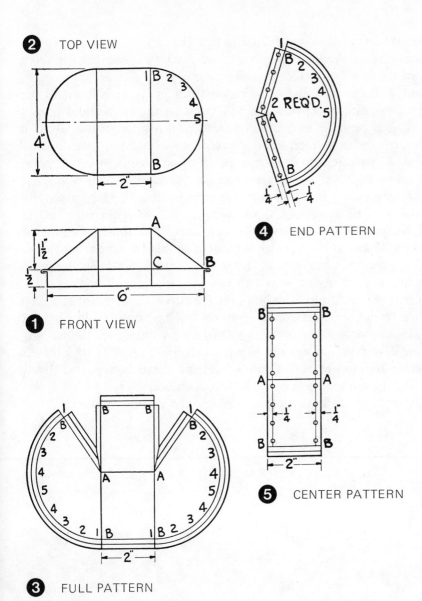

2 TOP VIEW

4"

2"

1 FRONT VIEW

1½"

½"

6"

3 FULL PATTERN

2"

4 END PATTERN

2 REQ'D.

¼" ¼"

5 CENTER PATTERN

2"

¼" ¼"

PLATE 87   ROUND OFFSET TAPER JOINT

Draw the front view or the cone profile so that the top opening is off center to the dimensions, as shown in Figures 1 and 2. Draw a straight line from the base points 1 and 7 to cross through points 1 and 7 at the top, to intersect at point A. Draw a straight line down from point A to intersect the base line 1–7 at point B. Divide the half circle at the base line 1–7 into equal spaces. Use point B as a center to draw an arc from each division point on the half circle, to intersect the base line 1–7.

Use point A as a center to draw a large arc from each intersecting point at the base line 1 to 7. Set the dividers to span the width of any one space in Figure 3 (representing one fourth of the circumference). Place one point of the dividers on the arc drawn from point 1 and swing the other leg to cross arc 2. Swing the dividers again to cross arc 3. Continue swinging the dividers from one arc to the next until enough spaces have been set out to equal the full circumference as from 1 to 7 and 7 to 1 shown in Figure 2. Draw a freehand curve from points 1 to 1.

Draw a straight line from each point on the curve 1–1 to point A. Draw a straight line from each intersecting point on the base line 1–7 in Figure 1 to point A. Use point A as a center, and draw an arc from each intersecting point on line 1–7 representing the top diameter in Figure 1, to intersect their respective lines in Figure 2. Draw a freehand curve from points 1 to 1, thus obtaining the circumference for the top diameter.

Make the necessary allowances to complete the pattern as shown.

PLATE 87

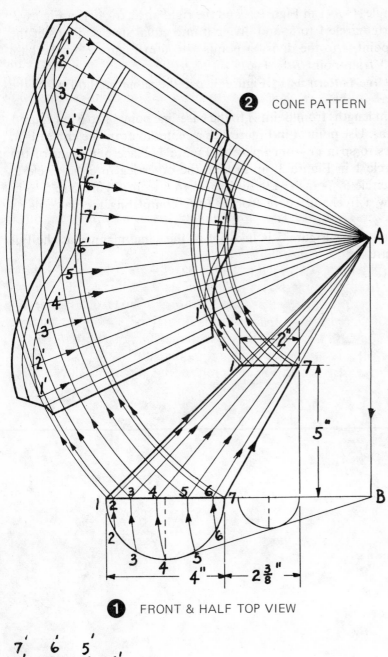

2 CONE PATTERN

1 FRONT & HALF TOP VIEW

5"

2"

7

5"

B

1   2   3   4   5   6   7
2   3   4   5   6
4"   2 3/8"

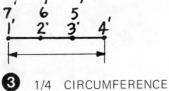

7'   6'   5'
1'   2'   3'   4'

3 1/4 CIRCUMFERENCE

PLATE 88   OBLONG HCOD OR COVER

Draw the triangle A–B–1 in Figure 1, and the right angle 6–A–1 in Figure 2. Draw the quarter circle 1 to 5, and divide it into equal spaces. Transfer the lengths from point A to the division points 1 to 6 in Figure 2, to the base line in Figure 1 from point B to 1–6.

To lay out the pattern as in Figure 3, use the same method as in the previous plate.

Use the slant lengths from point A to the base-line points 1 to 6 in Figure 1 as radius lengths. Use point A in Figure 3 as a center to draw the circles 1–6. Set the dividers to span any one space in Figure 4. Place one point of the dividers on circle 1 in Figure 3, and swing the other leg to cross circle 2, continuing to circle 5. Transfer the distance 5 to 6 from Figure 2 to 5–6 in Figure 3. Draw a freehand curve from 1 to 6, completing the patterns as shown.

The half pattern in Figure 5 is laid out in the same manner as the full pattern in Figure 3.

PLATE 88

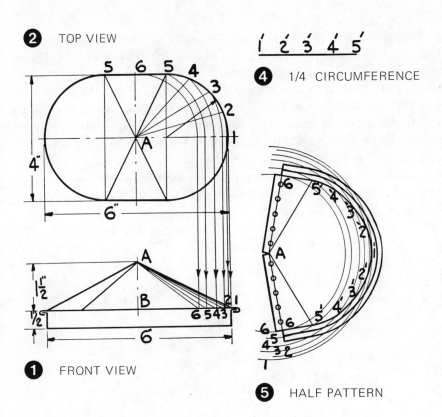

② TOP VIEW

4"

6"

① FRONT VIEW

④ 1/4 CIRCUMFERENCE

1' 2' 3' 4' 5'

⑤ HALF PATTERN

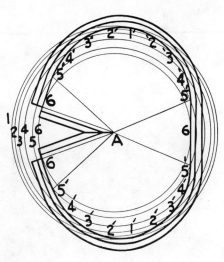

③ FULL PATTERN

PLATE 89   ELLIPTICAL-SHAPED HOOD OR COVER

The same method used in the previous plate may be used for this plate.

Draw the triangle *A–B–*1 in Figure 1, and the right angle 7*–A–*1 in Figure 2. Transfer the lengths from point *A* to points 1–7 in Figure 2, to the base line from *B* to 1–7 in Figure 1. Use the slant lengths from *A* to points 1–7 on the base line in Figure 1 as radius lengths. Use *A* in Figure 3 as a center, and draw the circles 1–7. Set the dividers to span any one space in Figure 2. Swing the dividers from circles 1 to 7 and 7 to 1 in Figure 3 in the same manner as in the previous plate.

Draw the freehand curve, and complete the pattern as shown.

The half pattern in Figure 4 is laid out by the same method as in Figure 3.

PLATE 89

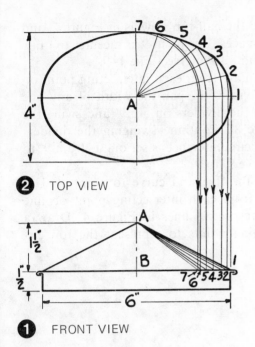

2 TOP VIEW

1 FRONT VIEW

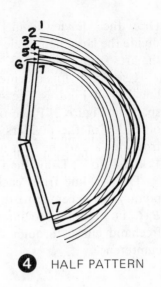

4 HALF PATTERN

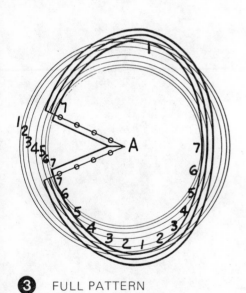

3 FULL PATTERN

PLATE 90   ROUND TAPER WITH ONE SIDE STRAIGHT

Draw the side view as in Figure 1, and the half-top view as in Figure 2, and divide the large half circle into equal spaces. Use point 9 as a center to draw the arcs from points 2, 3, 4, 5, 6, 7, and 8 to intersect line 1–9.

Use point *A* as a center to draw an arc from each intersecting point on line 1–9 in Figures 1 to 4. Set the dividers to span the width of any one space in Figure 3. Place one point of the dividers on arc 9′ and swing the other leg of the dividers to cross arc 8′. Continue swinging the dividers from one arc to the next until the full circumference is set out as from 9′ to 1′ and 1′ to 9′. Draw the freehand curve 9′ to 9′.

Draw a line from each point on the freehand curve to point *A*. Use point *A* as a center to draw an arc from each intersecting point on line *B–C* in Figure 1, to intersect their respective lines in Figure 4. Draw a freehand curve through the intersecting points to represent the top circumference.

PLATE 90

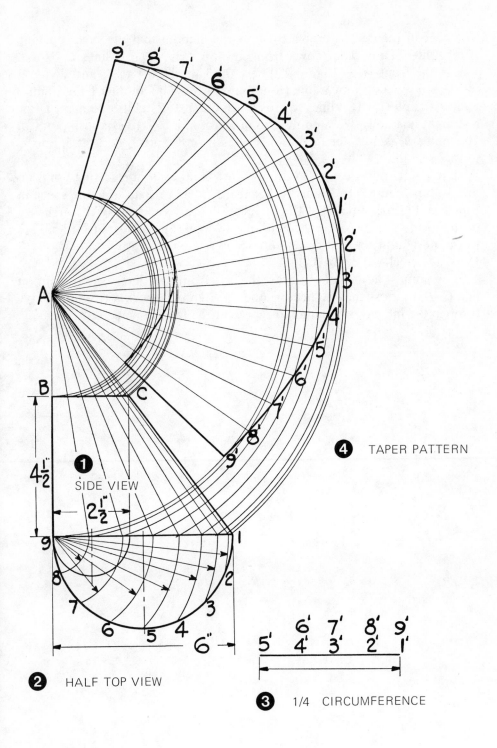

① SIDE VIEW

$4\frac{1}{2}''$

$2\frac{1}{2}''$

$6''$

② HALF TOP VIEW

④ TAPER PATTERN

③ 1/4 CIRCUMFERENCE

PLATE 91   ROUND TAPER OFF CENTER

The view in Figure 1 is drawn to show the amount that the small opening is off center. Draw lines down from the top view to cross lines $C-D$ and 1–7 in the front view, Figure 2. Draw the half circle 1 to 7, and divide it into equal spaces. Draw a line from point 1 to C and another from point 7 to D. Continue the two lines to cross each other, to establish point A. Draw a straight line down from point A to intersect line 1–7, to establish point B. Use point B as a center to draw the arcs from points 1, 2, 3, 4, 5, and 6, to intersect line 1–7.

Use point A as a center to draw an arc from each intersecting point on line 1–7 in Figure 2 to Figure 4. Set the dividers to span any one space in Figure 3. Place one point of the dividers on arc 1′, and swing the other leg of the dividers to cross arc 2′; continue swinging the dividers from one arc to the next until the full circumference is set out as 1′ to 7′ and 7′ to 1′. Draw the freehand curve 1′ to 1′.

Use point A as a center to draw the arcs from each intersecting point on line $C-D$, to cross their respective lines in Figure 4. Draw a freehand curve through the intersecting points to represent the top diameter.

PLATE 91

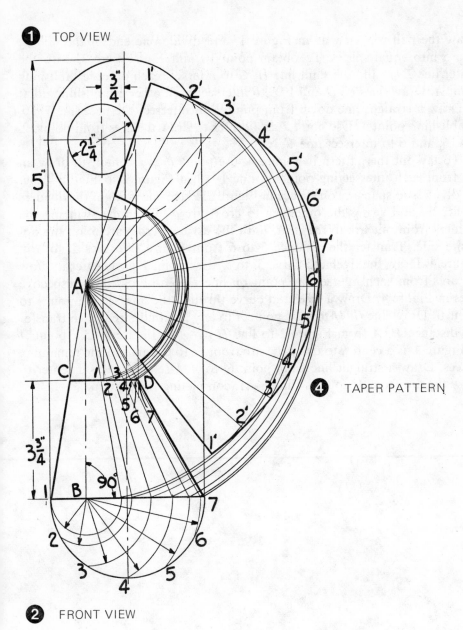

1 TOP VIEW

$\frac{3}{4}''$

$2\frac{1}{4}''$

5"

A

C

D

4 TAPER PATTERN

$3\frac{3}{4}''$

B   90°

2 FRONT VIEW

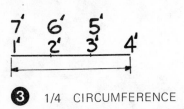

3 1/4 CIRCUMFERENCE

PLATE 92   OBLONG TO ROUND OFF CENTER

Draw the half-top view as in Figure 1, and divide one end of the oblong 1 to 5 into equal spaces. To obtain points A and F in Figure 2, draw the center line $B-D$ and the slant line $H-G$ to intersect each other, establishing point A. Draw lines $C-D$ and $1-E$ to intersect each other establishing point F. Draw a straight line down from point F to intersect the base line $1-10$, establishing point J. Use point J as a center to draw the arcs from points 2, 3, 4, 5, and 6 to intersect line $1-10$.

To lay out the pattern in Figure 4, use point F as a center, to draw an arc from each intersecting point on line $1-10$ in Figure 2 to Figure 4. Set the dividers to span any one space in Figure 3. Place one point of the dividers on arc $5'$, and swing the other leg to cross arc $4'$. Continue swinging the dividers from one arc to the next, until the dividers cross arc $5'$ on the opposite side. Transfer the distance 5 to 6 from Figure 1 to arcs $5'$ to 6 in Figure 4. Draw the freehand curve $5'$ to $5'$. Use point F as a center to draw the arcs from each intersecting point on line $E-G$ to cross their respective lines in Figure 4. Draw a freehand curve through the intersecting points to point G. Draw line $G-H$ toward point A to any length desired; then transfer the distance $H-A$ from Figure 2 to line $H-G-A$ in Figure 4. Use point A in Figure 4 as a center, to draw the arc from H to $6'$ equal to the remaining spaces. Draw a straight line from point $6'$ to A. Use point A as a center to draw the arc from H to cross line $6'-A$, completing the pattern.

PLATE 92

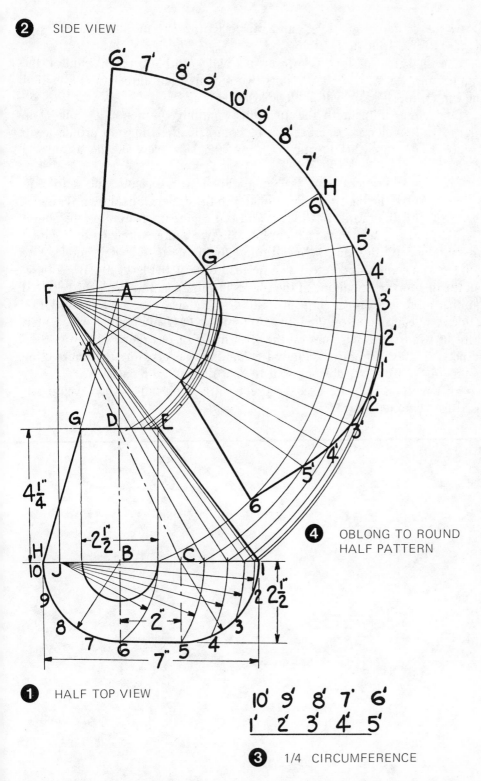

2 SIDE VIEW

4 OBLONG TO ROUND
HALF PATTERN

4 1/4"

2 1/2"

2 1/2"

2"

2"

7"

1 HALF TOP VIEW

10' 9' 8' 7' 6'
1' 2' 3' 4' 5'

3 1/4 CIRCUMFERENCE

153

PLATE 93   90-DEG. EQUAL-TAPERING ELBOW

Draw the center arc *A* to *E*, and divide it into the number of spaces as required for a four-piece elbow.

Use the same method as in previous plates on plain round elbows (the number of pieces times two, minus two, equals the number of spaces that the center line, 1 to 7, will be divided).

Draw lines tangent to the arc, thus obtaining points *B*, *C*, and *D* in Figure 1. It will not be necessary to complete the full side profile as in Figure 1, because this is only to show the side view of the assembled elbow.

Transfer the spaces *A* to *E* from Figure 1 to the center line *A* to *E* in Figure 2. Mark the base and top diameter to the dimensions shown. Transfer the angle and the radius of the first and last segments in Figure 1 to obtain the base and top segments in Figure 2. The two center segments in Figure 2 are obtained by drawing a line through point *C* at a 15-deg. angle. Use point *F* as a center, and *F* to 1 as a radius, to draw the large arc at the base. Set the dividers to equal one of the spaces in Figure 4, and mark the required number of spaces on the large arc 4 to 4 to equal the circumference. Draw a line from each point on the large arc to point *F*. Using point *F* as a center, draw an arc from each point on the slant line *F–1* in Figure 2 to cross their respective lines in Figure 3. Draw freehand curves crossing the intersecting points in Figure 3, which represent the cut lines for the patterns.

This method may be used very efficiently, especially when welding is used for seaming.

PLATE 93

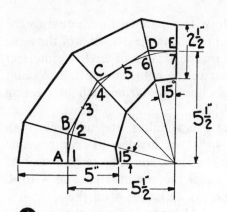

1 SIDE PROFILE

1 2 3 4

4 1/4 CIRCUMFERENCE

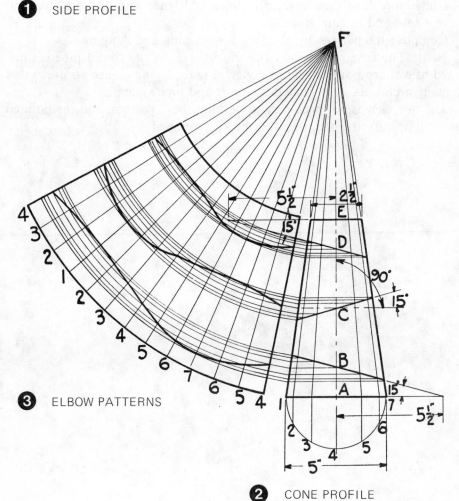

3 ELBOW PATTERNS

2 CONE PROFILE

PLATE 94 **TAPERING T INTERSECTING A ROUND PIPE AT A 90-DEG. ANGLE**

Draw the front view as in Figure 1. Draw two parallel lines equal to the diameter of the T to intersect the circle representing the diameter of the pipe. Draw straight lines from points 2 and 3 on the small half circle to intersect line 1–1. Draw a slant line from each intersecting point on line 1–1 to point A, crossing the large circle. Draw a straight line across from each intersecting point on the large circle to intersect line 1–A.

Use the slant length 1 to A in Figure 1 as a radius, and use point A in Figure 3 as a center to draw the arc at 4. Set the dividers to span any one space on the small half circle in Figure 1. Mark the required number of spaces on the large arc in Figure 3 to equal the circumference as 4 to 4. Transfer the lengths from point A to points 2, 3, and 4 on the slant line 1–A in Figure 1 to their respective lines in Figure 3. Draw the freehand curve 4 to 4 and the arc B–B.

Complete the pattern by allowing for seaming and flanging.

NOTE: The base of the intersection of the T on the round pipe is illustrated as a sharp point in the side view, Figure 2, and is also so illustrated by many architects when they design a round pipe system.

The side view is not necessary to develop the T pattern, and the pointed base will be curved when the side view is developed.

PLATE 94

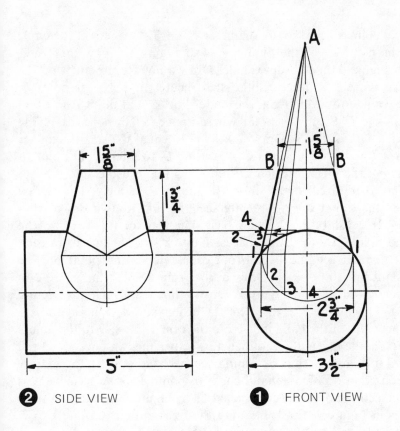

2 SIDE VIEW

1 FRONT VIEW

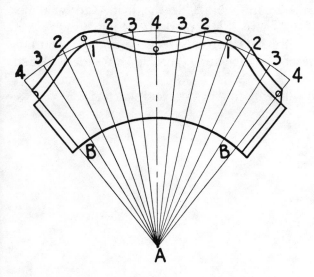

3 TAPERING TEE PATTERN

PLATE 95 TAPERING T INTERSECTING A ROUND PIPE
AT A 45-DEG. ANGLE

Draw two parallel lines equal to the diameter of the T, to intersect the circle representing the diameter of the pipe at 4–4 in Figure 1. Draw the center line A–B–4 in Figure 2 on a 45-deg. angle. Draw a line from point 4 on the large circle in Figure 1 to intersect the slant center line A–4 at point B, Figure 2. Draw a line squaring from the center line A–4 at point B to equal the diameter of the T. From the point where the center line A crosses line E–F, mark the length of the T. Draw line C–C to equal the small diameter of the T. Draw a line through points C–4′ and C–D, to intersect at point A. Continue drawing the lines through D and 4′ as far into the side view of the pipe as may be desired, or as shown in Figure 2, namely, 1 in. Draw line 1–7 across the center line A, to intersect the lines drawn down from C–D and C–4, thus establishing a new base diameter for the T. Draw the half circle, and divide it into equal spaces. Draw a straight line from each division point to intersect line 1–7. From each intersecting point on line 1–7, draw a slant line to point A. Draw a line from point A in Figure 2 to intersect the center line at A in Figure 1. Draw a line from each intersecting point on line 1–7 in Figure 2 to intersect the center line A–7 in Figure 1.

Transfer the width of the half circle from the center line 1–7 to the points 2–6 on the curved line in Figure 2 to their respective lines on one side of the center line A–7 in Figure 1, thus obtaining the freehand curve 1 to 7. Draw a line from each point on the freehand curve to point A. Draw a line across from each intersecting point on the large circle in Figure 1 to intersect their respective lines in Figure 2, thus obtaining the freehand curved line 1 to 7. Draw a line parallel to line C–C from each point on the freehand curve to intersect the slant line A–1 in Figure 2. Use the slant length A to 1 in Figure 2 as a radius, and draw the large arc in Figure 3. Set the dividers to equal any one space on the half circle in Figure 2, and mark the required number of spaces 7 to 7 on the arc in Figure 3. Transfer the lengths from the slant line A–1 in Figure 2 to their respective lines in Figure 3. Draw the freehand curve and the arc C–C.

Complete the pattern by allowing for seaming and flanging.

PLATE 95

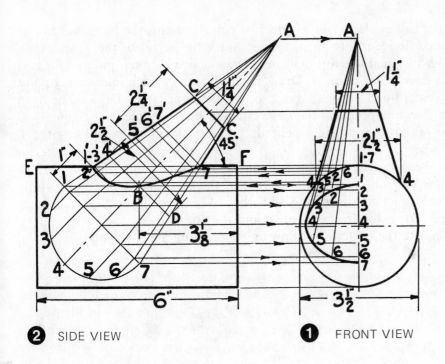

2 SIDE VIEW

1 FRONT VIEW

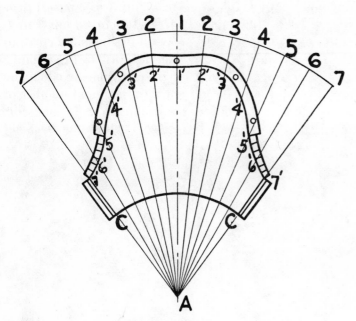

3 TAPERING TEE PATTERN

PLATE 96   TAPERING T INTERSECTING A ROUND
PIPE OFF CENTER

Draw the half circle 1–7 in Figure 1, which represents the base diameter of the T, and divide it into equal spaces. Mark the height of the T, and draw line $B–B$ to equal the top diameter. Draw a line through points 7–B and 1–B, to intersect at point A. Draw a slant line from each intersecting point on the center line 1–7 to point A, crossing the large circle. Draw a line from each intersecting point on the large circle to intersect line $A–7$. Point $7'–C$ may be raised to any height desired. This is to facilitate connecting the T to the pipe.

Use the slant length A to 7 in Figure 1 as a radius, and draw the arc 1–1 in Figure 3 equal to the circumference of the small half circle in Figure 1. Transfer the lengths from the slant line $A–7$ to their respective lines in Figure 3. Draw the freehand curve and the arc $B–B$.

Complete the pattern by allowing for seaming and flanging.

PLATE 96

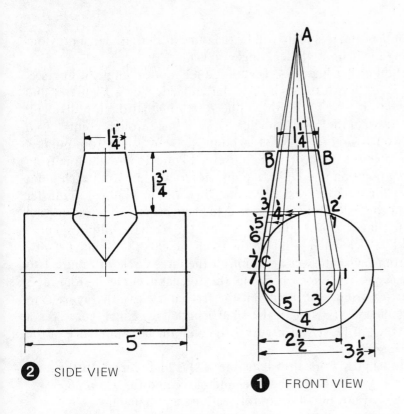

2 SIDE VIEW

1 FRONT VIEW

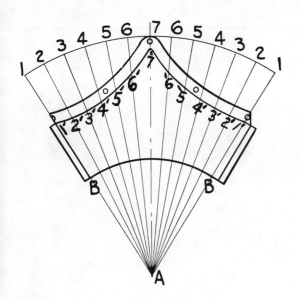

3 TAPERING TEE PATTERN

PLATE 97   TAPERING T ON A 45-DEG. ANGLE OFF CENTER

The method for drawing this plate will be the same as that used in a previous plate illustrating the T on a 45-deg. angle on center.

Draw the slant center line A–4, Figure 2, on a 45-deg. angle to intersect the center line C–C drawn through the front and side views, Figures 1 and 2. Mark the length of the T, and draw line B–B to equal the top diameter and line $1E$–7 to equal the base diameter. Draw a line through points $1E$–B and another through 7–B to intersect at point A. Draw a line from point A in Figure 2 to intersect the center line at A in Figure 1. Draw a line from each intersecting point on line $1E$–7 to point A. Draw a line from each point on line $1E$–7 in Figure 2 to cross the center line A–7 in Figure 1. Transfer the widths from the half circle in Figure 2 to their respective lines on each side of the center line A–7 in Figure 1 to obtain the freehand elliptical curve 1 to 7. Draw a line from each point on the freehand curve to point A. Draw a line across from each intersecting point on the large circle in Figure 1 to intersect their respective lines obtaining the freehand curve in Figure 2. Draw a line across from each point on the freehand curve in Figure 2 to intersect the slant line $1E$–A. Use the slant length $1E$–A in Figure 2 as a radius to draw the arc $1E$–$1E$ in Figure 3 to equal the circumference of the half circle in Figure 2.

Transfer the lengths from the slant line A–$1E$ in Figure 2 to their respective lines in Figure 3. Draw the freehand curve and the arc B–B.

Complete the pattern by allowing for seaming and flanging.

PLATE 97

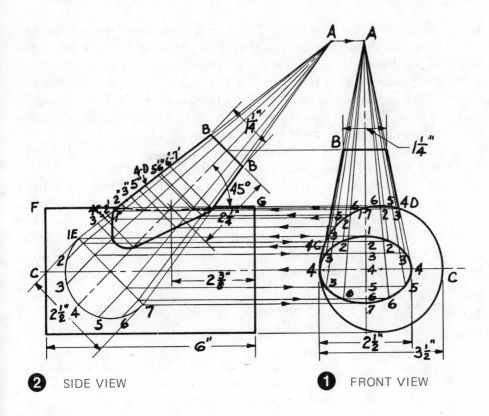

2 SIDE VIEW

1 FRONT VIEW

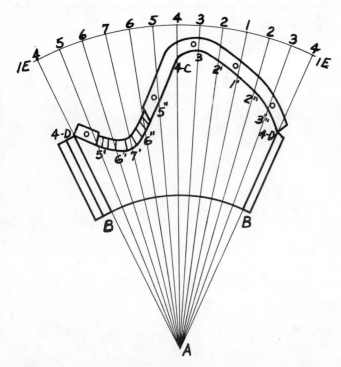

3 TEE PATTERN

PLATE 98   SQUARE TAPERING T INTERSECTING A

ROUND PIPE ON CENTER

Draw the width of the base of the T to intersect the circle representing the round pipe, and divide it into equal spaces, as shown in Figure 1. Mark the height of the T and the width of the top to the dimensions as shown. Draw a line from each division point on line 1–1 to point A. Complete the full square. Then use the distance C to B as a radius and point B as a center to draw arc C–D. Draw a straight line up from D to $1E$. Draw a line from the intersecting points on the circle to the slant line A–$1E$.

Use the slant length A to $1E$ in Figure 1 as a radius to draw the large arc $1E$ in Figure 3. Transfer the width 1 to 1 from Figure 1 to the arc $1E$–$1E$ in Figure 3, and draw straight lines connecting each point. Draw a line from each point on the straight base line $1E$ to point A. Transfer the lengths from line A–$1E$ in Figure 1 to each corner line represented by $1E$ in Figure 3. Draw straight lines connecting each point on line A–$1E$, crossing their respective lines drawn from the base line to point A, thus obtaining the free-hand curve $1E$ to $1E$ on two sides. Use the distance A to F in Figure 1 as a radius to draw the arc F–F in Figure 3.

Complete the pattern by allowing for seaming and flanging.

PLATE 98

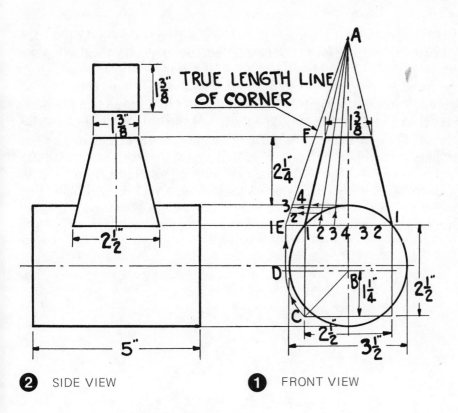

2 SIDE VIEW

1 FRONT VIEW

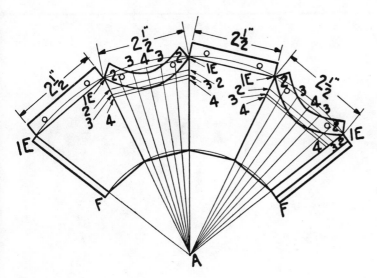

3 TEE PATTERN

PLATE 99   SQUARE TAPERING T INTERSECTING A

ROUND PIPE OFF CENTER

Draw the front view as in Figure 1, using the same method as in the previous plate. Point 1 may be raised to the height desired to facilitate connecting the T to the pipe.

Use the slant length A to $1E$ in Figure 1 as a radius to draw the arc $1E$ in Figure 3. Transfer the width 1 to 7 from Figure 1 to the arc $1E$ in Figure 3. Connect each point, and draw a line from each division point on the base to point A. Transfer the lengths on the slant line A–$1E$ in Figure 1 to the corner lines represented by $1E$ in Figure 3. Draw straight lines connecting each point on line A–$1E$, crossing their respective lines drawn from the base line to point A, thus obtaining the freehand curve 1 to 7 on two sides. Use the distance A to F in Figure 1 as a radius to draw arc F in Figure 3.

Complete the pattern by allowing for seaming and flanging.

PLATE 99

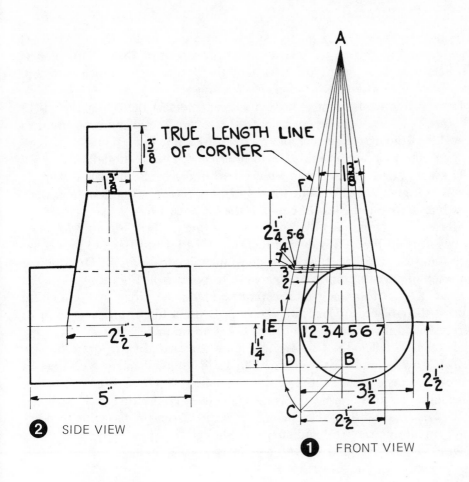

TRUE LENGTH LINE OF CORNER

2 SIDE VIEW

1 FRONT VIEW

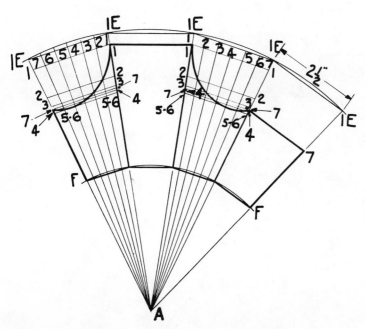

3 TEE PATTERN

PLATE 100   SQUARE TAPERING T ON A 45-DEG.

ANGLE ON CENTER

Draw the center line $A-B$ in Figure 2 on a 45-deg. angle. Draw line $C-D$ perpendicular to the center line to equal the width of the T, until line C intersects line $E-F$. Mark the length of the T and the width at the top. Draw lines from C and D to intersect at point A.

Draw a line from point A in Figure 2 to intersect the center line $A-13$ in Figure 1. Draw two lines parallel to the center line in Figure 1 equal to the width of the T to intersect line $E-F$. Draw a line from point A through the intersecting points on line $E-F$ to intersect the circle at 4–4.

Draw a line from point 4 in Figure 1 to intersect the slant line $A-C$ at point 4 in Figure 2. Draw a line from 4 to 10 to intersect the slant line $A-D$. Draw lines 4 to 1 and 10 to 13 equal to the distance 4 to B.

Draw a line from each division point on line 4–10 in Figure 2 to intersect line 4–10 in Figure 1. Divide the distance 1 to 4 and 10 to 13 into equal spaces, and draw a line from each division point to point A. Draw a line from each intersecting point on line 4–10 to point A in Figure 1.

Draw a line from each intersecting point on the circle in Figure 1 to intersect their respective lines in Figure 2. Draw a line from each point of intersection to intersect the slant line $A-4H$ and number each.

Use the slant length A to $4H$ in Figure 2 as a radius to draw the arc $4H$ in Figure 3. Transfer the spaces 1 to 13 in Figure 2 to the base lines in Figure 3. Transfer the lengths on the slant line $A-4H$ in Figure 2 to the corner lines $4H$ in Figure 3. Draw straight lines connecting each point on line $A-4H$, crossing their respective lines drawn from the base line to point A, thus obtaining the freehand curves as shown.

Draw the arc $J-J$ and allow for seaming and flanging.

PLATE 100

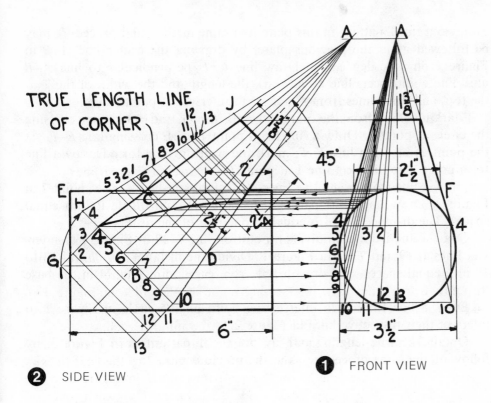

TRUE LENGTH LINE
OF CORNER

45°

2"

$2\frac{1}{2}$"

$1\frac{3}{8}$"

6"

$3\frac{1}{2}$"

2 SIDE VIEW

1 FRONT VIEW

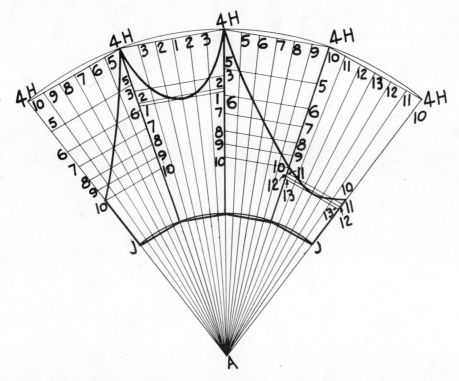

3 TEE PATTERN

PLATE 101 **SQUARE TAPERING T ON A 45-DEG.**

ANGLE OFF CENTER

To lay out the T pattern in this plate, the same method and procedure may be followed as in the previous plate, by drawing the center line $A-B$ in Figure 2 on a 45-deg. angle. Draw line $C-D$ perpendicular to line $A-B$ until line C intersects line $E-F$. Mark the length and the width of the T at the top, and draw lines from C and D to intersect at point A.

Mark up $\frac{1}{2}$ in. from the center line in Figure 1, and draw a line crossing the circle at point 1. Draw a line from point 1 to A, crossing line $E-F$. At the point of crossing line $E-F$, mark the width of the T, and draw a line from point A to intersect line 1 at point 7.

Draw a line from point 1 in Figure 1 to intersect line $A-C$ at point 7 in Figure 2. Draw line 7–13 parallel to line $C-D$, and divide it into equal spaces. The distance 7 to 4 is equal to one half of the distance 7–13.

Draw a line from each division point on line 7–13 in Figure 2 to intersect lines 1–19 and 7–13 in Figure 1. Divide the distance 1 to 7 and 13 to 19 into equal spaces, and draw a line from each point 1 to 24 in the base to point A.

Draw a line from each intersecting point on the circle in Figure 1 to intersect their respective lines in Figure 2.

Obtain the true lengths, and lay out the T pattern as in Figure 3, by following the same procedure as in the previous plate.

PLATE 101

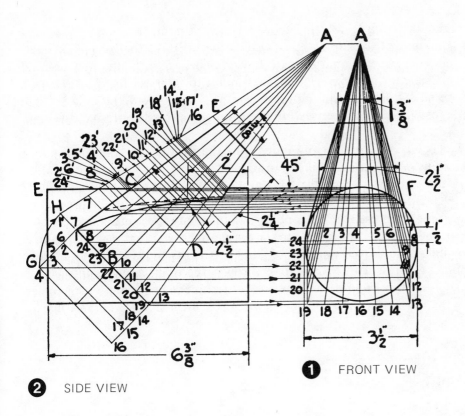

1 FRONT VIEW

2 SIDE VIEW

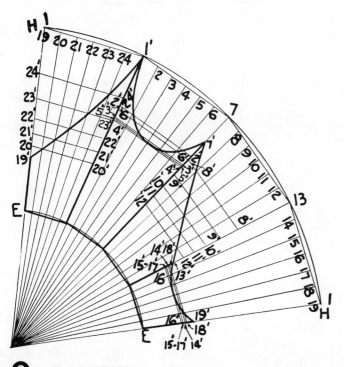

3 TEE PATTERN

To obtain the front view as in Figure 1, draw the circle for the pipe diameter and the width of the top B–B, as well as the width of the base $5'$–5, intersecting the circle at a quarter turn. Divide line $1'$–$5'$ into equal spaces, and draw a straight line from each division point to intersect line $5'$–5. Draw a line from each intersecting point on line $5'$–5 to point A. Draw a straight line across from each intersecting point on the circle to intersect the slant line A–$5'$.

To lay out the T pattern in Figure 3, use the slant length A to 5 in Figure 1 as a radius. Then, using A in Figure 3 as a center, draw the large arc 1–1. Mark the widths 1 to 5 on the large arc to represent the four sides of the T; divide each into the same number of spaces as line 1–$5'$ in Figure 1; and draw a line from each division point 1–5 to point A. Transfer the spaces A to $5'$ from line A–$5'$ in Figure 1 to the corner lines A–1 and A–5 in Figure 3. Draw lines across from points $2'$, $3'$, and $4'$, to cross lines 2, 3, and 4 drawn to point A. Draw a freehand curve through the intersecting points 1 to 5. Using A to B in Figure 1 as a radius, and point A in Figure 3 as a center, draw the arc B–B. Draw straight lines across from 1 to 5, completing the T pattern.

PLATE 102

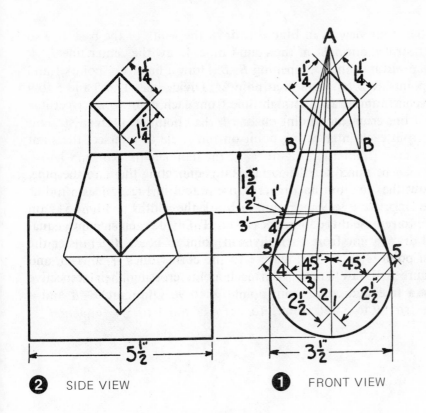

2 SIDE VIEW

1 FRONT VIEW

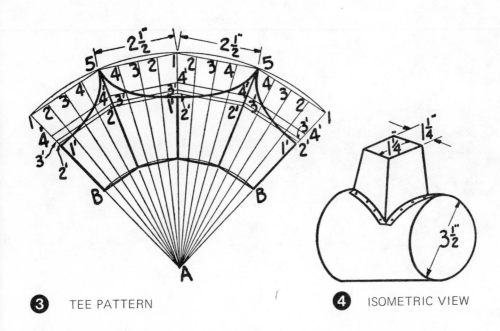

3 TEE PATTERN

4 ISOMETRIC VIEW

To obtain the front view as in Figure 1, draw the width of the base 1–9 so that point 1 strikes one side of the round pipe. Draw the center line 5–A, and mark the width of the top opening B–B. Draw a line from points 1 and 9 crossing points B–B to intersect at point A. Divide lines 1 to 5 and 5 to 9 into equal spaces, and draw a straight line from each point to intersect line 1–9. Draw a line from each point on line 1–9 to point A. Draw a straight line across from each intersecting point on the circle to intersect the slant line A–1.

Point 1 may be raised a trifle to facilitate connecting the T to the pipe.

To lay out the T pattern in Figure 3, use A to 1 in Figure 1 as a radius to draw the large arc 9 to 9 in Figure 3. Mark the widths 1–5 and 5–9 on the large arc to represent the four sides of the T. Divide each side into equal spaces, and draw a line from each division point to point A. Transfer the spaces from point A to 1A in Figure 1 to the corner lines A–9, A–5, and A–1 in Figure 3. Draw a line from each point crossing their respective lines. Draw a freehand curve from point 1A to 9′. Draw arc B–B and a straight line from 9 to 5 and from 5 to 1.

PLATE 103

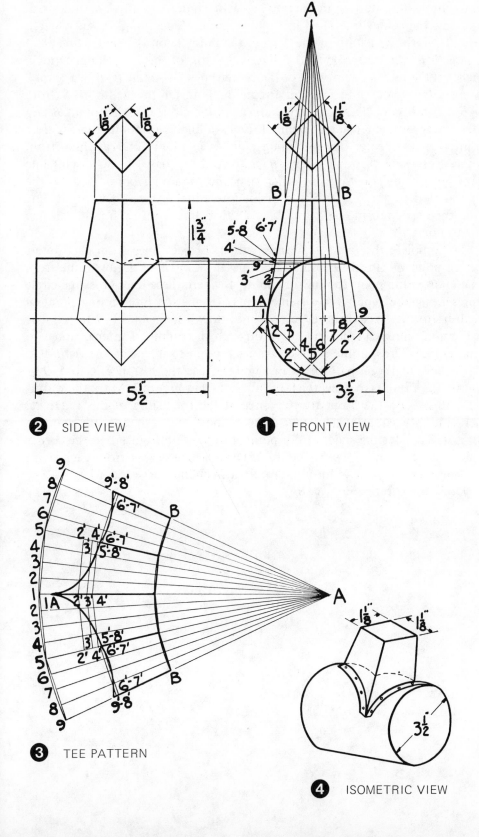

A

1⅛" 1⅛"

1⅛" 1⅛"

B   B   B   B

1¾"

5'-8' 6'-7'
4'
9'
3' 2'
5-8 6-7

1A
1
2 3 4 5 6 7 8 9
2"   2"

5½"   3½"

② SIDE VIEW   **①** FRONT VIEW

9
8
7
6
5
4
3
2
1A
2
3
4
5
6
7
8
9

9'-8'
6'-7'   B
2' 4' 6'-7'
3' 5'-8'
2'3'4'
3' 5'-8'
2' 4' 6'-7'
6'-7'   B
9'-8'

A

1⅛"   1⅛"

3½"

③ TEE PATTERN   **④** ISOMETRIC VIEW

175

PLATE 104   SQUARE TAPERING T AT 45 DEG.,

ONE-QUARTER TURN ON CENTER

Draw the center line 1–A in the front view in Figure 1 to any length desired.

Draw the center line D–A in Figure 2 on a 45-deg. angle to any length desired. Mark the length of the T from the point C on the center line D–A to line B–B which represents the diagonal width of the T opening. Draw a line from the intersecting point of the center lines D–A and B–B in Figure 2 to cross the center line D–A in Figure 1. Transfer the width B–B from Figure 2 to Figure 1. Draw a line tangent to the circle crossing point B and intersecting the center line at point A. Draw a line from point A in Figure 1 to intersect the center line obtaining point A in Figure 2; draw lines from point A crossing through points B–B toward the base; draw a slant line from point 9 intersecting the other side line obtaining point 1; draw the right angle 1 to 5 and 5 to 9, and divide into equal spaces, then draw a line from each space to intersect line 1–9. Draw a line from each point on line 1–9 to point A.

To complete the front view in Figure 1, project lines from each intersecting point on line 1–9 to intersect lines 1–5 and 5–9. Draw a line from each intersecting point to intersect point A, where these lines cross the circle representing the pipe. Draw a line across from each intersecting point in Figure 1 to intersect their respective lines drawn from line 1–9 to point A in Figure 2. Draw a freehand curve through the points of intersection 1 to 5 and 5 to 9. Draw a line across from each point to intersect line A–B–9.

To lay out the T pattern as in Figure 3, use the distance A to 5–9 in Figure 2 as a radius to draw the large arc 1–5–9 in Figure 3. Mark the widths 1–5 and 5–9 on the large arc to represent the four sides of the T. Divide each side into equal spaces, and draw a line from each division point to point A. Transfer the spaces from point A to 5′–9′ in Figure 2 to the corner lines A–1, A–5, and A–9 in Figure 3. Draw a line across from each point crossing their respective lines, and draw a freehand curve from 1 to 9.

Draw the top opening B–B.

PLATE 104

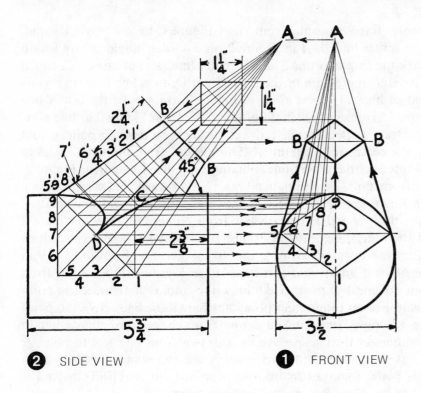

$1\frac{1}{4}"$

$1\frac{1}{4}"$

A A

B

B B

B B

45°

B

$2\frac{1}{4}"$

7' 6' 4' 3' 2' 1'

5' 9' 8' 1'

9

8

7

6

5 3

4 2 1

C

D

$2\frac{3}{8}"$

9

5 6 7 8 D

4 3

2

1

$5\frac{3}{4}"$

$3\frac{1}{2}"$

② SIDE VIEW

① FRONT VIEW

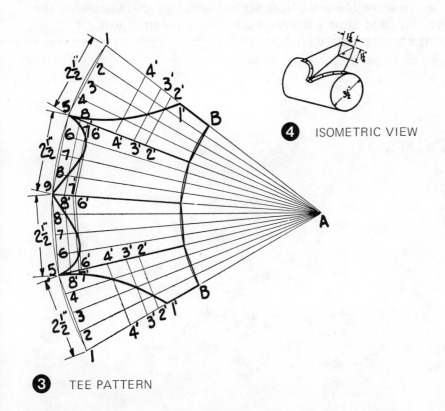

1

$2\frac{1}{2}"$ 2

5 4 3

8

6

$2\frac{1}{2}"$ 7

8

9

8

7

$2\frac{1}{2}"$ 6

5

4

8'

$2\frac{1}{2}"$ 3

2

1

4' 3' 2'

8

6 16 4 3 2

7

6'

6'

6' 4' 3' 2'

6'

8'

4

B

1'

B

A

B

③ TEE PATTERN

$1\frac{1}{4}$

$1\frac{1}{4}$

$3\frac{1}{2}"$

④ ISOMETRIC VIEW

177

PLATE 105

SQUARE TAPERING T AT 45 DEG., ONE-QUARTER TURN OFF CENTER

Draw the center line 9–A in the front view, Figure 1, to any length desired.

Draw the center line D–A in Figure 2 on a 45 deg. angle to any length desired. Mark the length of the T on the center line D–A at line C–C, which represents the diagonal width of the T opening. Draw a line from the intersecting point of lines D–A and C–C in Figure 2 to intersect the center line 9–A in Figure 1. Transfer the length of line C–C from Figure 2 to line C–C in Figure 1. Draw a line tangent to the circle crossing through point C and intersecting the center line at point A. Draw a line from points A and 5 in Figure 1 to intersect the center line, obtaining points A and D in Figure 2. Draw lines from point A through points C–C toward the base. Draw a slant line through point D to intersect the lines drawn down from point A, obtaining points 1–B and 5. Draw a line from points 1B and 9 in Figure 2 to intersect the center line A–D in Figure 1, to establish points 1–9, which represent the base opening. Draw a line from each point on line 1B–9 in Figure 2 to intersect lines 1–5–9, and 9–13–1 in Figure 1. Draw a line from each intersecting point to point A. Draw a line from each intersecting point on the circle in Figure 1 to intersect the lines drawn from line 1B–9 to point A in Figure 2. Draw a line from each point on the freehand curved line to intersect line 1B–A.

To lay out the T pattern as in Figure 3, use the same procedure as in the previous plate, by constructing the base line 1B to 1B. Transfer the spaces from point A to 1B in Figure 2 to the corner lines 1B–A, 5–A, 9–A, and 13–A in Figure 3. Draw a line across from each point, crossing their respective lines, and draw a freehand curve from points 1′ to 1′.

Draw the top opening B–B.

PLATE 105

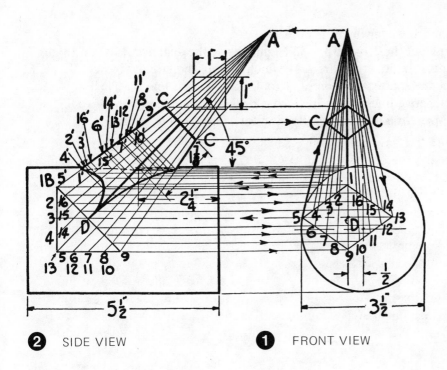

2 SIDE VIEW

1 FRONT VIEW

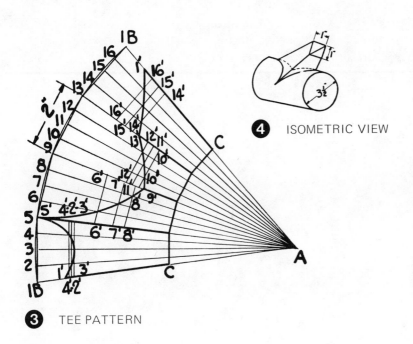

3 TEE PATTERN

4 ISOMETRIC VIEW

**PLATE 106   ROUND TAPERING T INTERSECTING CYLINDER
AT 90 DEG.**

Draw the front view as in Figure 1.

To lay out the T pattern as in Figure 3, use the distance *A* to 1 in Figure 1 as a radius to draw the arc 4–4 which equals the circumference of the T. Transfer the spaces from point *A* to 4′ on the slant line *A*–1 in Figure 1 to their respective lines in Figure 3, and draw the freehand curve 4 to 4.

Complete the pattern by allowing for seaming and flanging.

PLATE 106

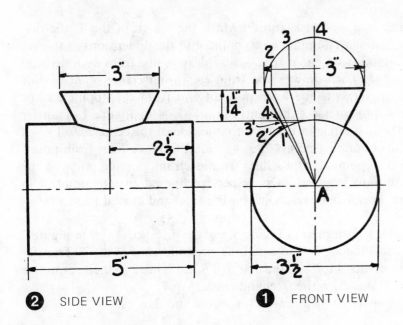

② SIDE VIEW   **①** FRONT VIEW

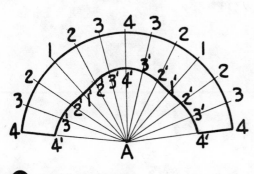

③ TEE PATTERN

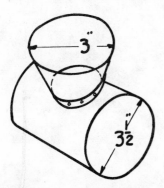

④ ISOMETRIC VIEW

PLATE 107   ROUND TAPERING T AT 45 DEG. ON CENTER

Draw the center line A–4 in Figure 2. Mark the length of the T, the diameter, and the distance from line $1B$ to point A to the dimensions as shown. Divide the half circle into equal spaces, and draw a line from each division point to line $1B$–7. Then draw a line from each intersecting point on line $1B$–7 to point A. Draw a line from point A and from each point on line $1B$–7 in Figure 2 to intersect the center line 1–7–A in Figure 1. Transfer the widths of the half circle in Figure 2 to one side of the center line 1–7–A in Figure 1, thus obtaining points 2, 3, 4, 5, and 6. Draw lines from points 2, 3, 4, 5, and 6 to point A. Draw lines from each intersecting point on the circle in Figure 1 to intersect their respective lines drawn to point A in Figure 2. Draw lines from each point on the freehand curved line to intersect line A–1B.

To lay out the T pattern as in Figure 3, use the distance A–1B in Figure 2 as a radius to draw the arc 7–7 to equal the circumference of the T. Transfer the spaces from points A to 7′ on the line A–1B in Figure 2 to their respective lines in Figure 3, and draw the freehand curve 7 to 7.

Complete the pattern by allowing for seams and flanges.

PLATE 107

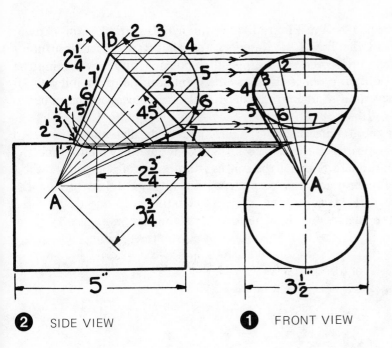

2 SIDE VIEW   **1** FRONT VIEW

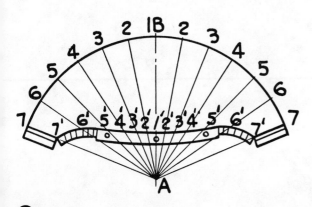

3 TEE PATTERN

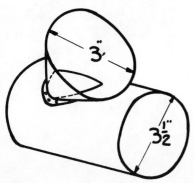

4 ISOMETRIC VIEW

183

PLATE 108   ROUND TAPERING T AT 90 DEG. OFF CENTER

Draw the center line A–4 in Figure 1 off center as to the dimensions shown; also the height of the T and the diameter $1B$–$7B$. Draw a line from point $7B$, striking the round pipe on a tangent at point $7'$ and intersecting the center line 4 to obtain point A. Draw a line from each point on line $1B$–$7B$ to point A; then draw a line from each intersecting point on the circle to intersect line A–$7B$.

To lay out the T pattern as in Figure 3, use the distance A to $7B$ in Figure 1 as a radius to draw the arc $1B$–$1B$ in Figure 3, which equals the circumference of the T. Transfer the spaces from points A to $1'$ on the slant line A–$7B$ in Figure 1 to their respective lines in Figure 3, to obtain the freehand curve $1'$ to $1'$.

Complete the pattern by allowing for seams and flanges.

PLATE 108

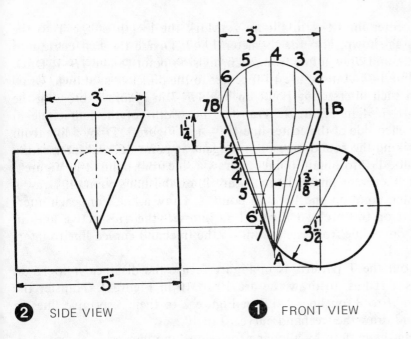

2 SIDE VIEW

1 FRONT VIEW

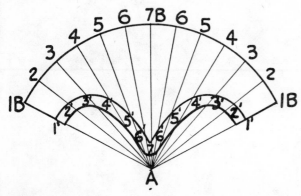

3 TEE PATTERN

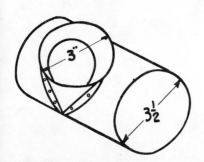

4 ISOMETRIC VIEW

185

PLATE 109   ROUND TAPERING T AT 45 DEG. OFF CENTER

Draw the center line A–4 in Figure 2. Mark the length of the T to the dimensions as shown, also the diameter 1B–7. Divide the half circle into equal spaces, and draw a line from each division point to line 1B–7. Draw the center line 1–7–A in Figure 1 off center to the dimensions shown. Draw a line from each intersecting point on line 1B–7 in Figure 2, crossing the center line 1–7–A in Figure 1. Transfer the widths of the half circle in Figure 2 to each side of the center line 1–7–A in Figure 1. Draw a line from point 4, striking the round pipe on a tangent at point 4C and intersecting the center line 1–7 to obtain point A. Draw a line from point A in Figure 1 to intersect the center line 4–10 in Figure 2, establishing point A. Draw a line from each point on line 1B–7 to point A. Draw a line from each intersecting point on the circle in Figure 1 to intersect their respective lines in Figure 2. Draw a line from each point on the freehand curved line to intersect line 1B–A.

To lay out the T pattern as in Figure 3, use the distance A to 1B in Figure 2 as a radius, to draw the arc 10 to 10 in Figure 3. Transfer the spaces from A to 8′ on line A–1B in Figure 2 to their respective lines in Figure 3, and draw the freehand curve 10 to 10.

Complete the pattern by allowing for seams and flanges.

PLATE 109

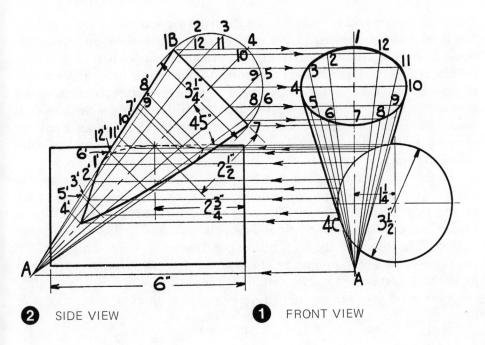

2 SIDE VIEW

1 FRONT VIEW

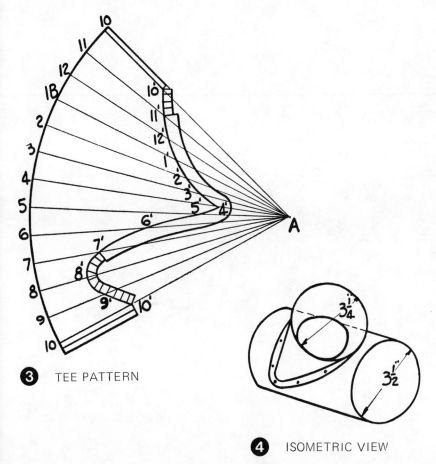

3 TEE PATTERN

4 ISOMETRIC VIEW

PLATE 110   SQUARE TAPERING T INTERSECTING THE HIP

OF A HOOD

Draw the top view as in Figure 1 and the front view as in Figure 2. Draw a line from point D in Figure 2, the intersecting point of the T and hip of the hood, to intersect the hip line in Figure 1, establishing point D'.

Use A to F in Figure 2 as a radius, and point A in Figure 3 as a center to draw the arc F to F. Mark four spaces on the arc, each equal to the width of one side of the T, and draw a line from each to point A. Use A to G in Figure 2 as a radius to draw the arc $G-G$ in Figure 3. Draw a slant line from points G to the first point on arc $F-F$. Draw arc $H-H$ to obtain the width of the top opening.

To lay out the end pattern as in Figure 4, draw the width of the base to the dimensions given, and the center line $B-E$ equal to the spaces B to E on the slant line in Figure 2. Transfer the widths $D-D'$ and $C-C'$ from Figure 1 to their respective lines in Figure 4.

Since the sides and the ends of the hood have the same slope or pitch, the patterns will be the same height, and the end pattern may be used to mark the T cutout on the side pattern.

Allowances for seaming and riveting may be as desired.

PLATE 110

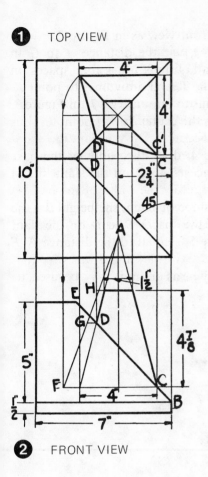

① TOP VIEW

② FRONT VIEW

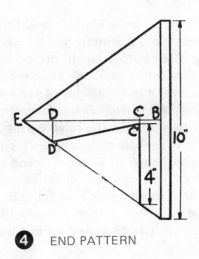

④ END PATTERN

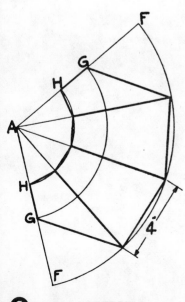

③ TEE PATTERN

Draw the top view as in Figure 1 and the front view as in Figure 2.

To lay out the T pattern as in Figure 3, use the distance A to G in Figure 2 as a radius to draw the arc G–G in Figure 3. Mark four spaces on arc G–G equal to the width of the base of the T, and draw lines to point A. Use the distance A to H in Figure 2 as a radius to draw arc H–H in Figure 3. Draw a straight line from H to H, crossing the center line at point E, thus obtaining the cutout for the ridge on the hood.

To lay out the end pattern as in Figure 4, draw the width of the base and the center line B to D equal to the spaces B to D on the slant line in Figure 2.

Since the sides and ends have the same slope or pitch, the height for the side pattern B to D in Figure 5 is equal to the spaces B to D on the slant line in Figure 2. The distance F–E in Figure 5 is equal to the distance F–E in Figure 2.

Allowances for seaming and riveting may be as desired.

PLATE 111

1 TOP VIEW

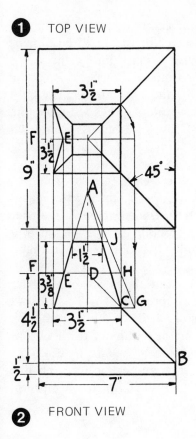

2 FRONT VIEW

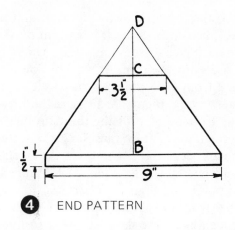

4 END PATTERN

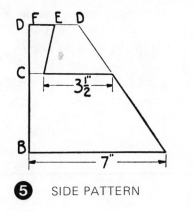

5 SIDE PATTERN

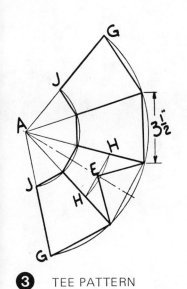

3 TEE PATTERN

PLATE 112 **ROUND TAPERING T INTERSECTING**

THE HIP OF A HOOD

Draw the top view as in Figure 1, and place the center of the T on the hip line. Then draw a circle representing the diameter of the T to the dimensions as given. Draw the front view as in Figure 2, mark the height of the T, and draw the slant lines from points $D-D$ to intersect at point A. Draw a line from each point on the circle 1 to 7 in Figure 1 to intersect the base line $D-D$ in Figure 2. Draw a line from each intersecting point on line $D-D$ to point A, crossing the slant line $B-C$. Draw a line across from each intersecting point on line $B-C$ to intersect the slant line $A-D$, and crossing their respective lines to obtain the freehand curve from 1' to 7'.

To lay out the T pattern as in Figure 3, use A to D in Figure 2 as a radius, and point A in Figure 3 as a center to draw the arc $D-D$. Transfer the spaces 1 to 7 from the circle in Figure 1 to the arc $D1$ to $D1$ in Figure 3. Transfer the lengths on the slant line $A-D$ from point A to points 1, 2, 3, 4, 5, 6, and 7 in Figure 2 to their respective lines in Figure 3 to obtain the freehand curve 1 to 7.

To lay out the side pattern as in Figure 4, draw the width of the base and transfer the spaces on the slant line $B-C$, represented by 1', 2', 3', 4', 5', 6', 7', and D in Figure 2, to line $B-C$ in Figure 4. Draw a line from each point on line $B-C$ to cross line $A-D'$. Transfer the widths of the T cutout from one side of the center line $A-D'$, represented by points 1'-1", 2'-2", 3'-3", 4'-4", 7"-7', and 5'-6' in Figure 2 to their respective lines on line $A-D'$ in Figure 4. Draw the freehand curve 1' to 7' to complete the pattern.

PLATE 112

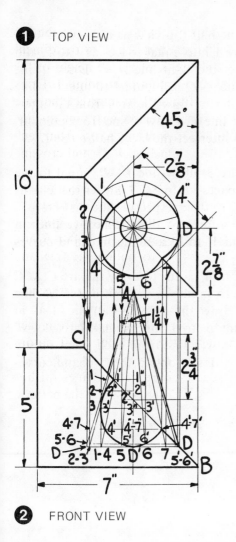

1 TOP VIEW

2 FRONT VIEW

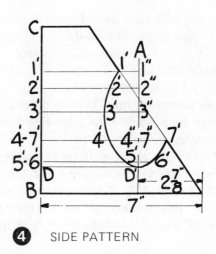

4 SIDE PATTERN

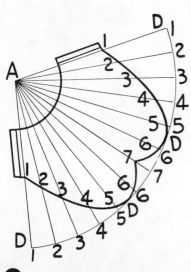

3 TEE PATTERN

193

PLATE 113   RECTANGULAR HORIZONTAL T ON A TAPER

Draw the side view as in Figure 1 and the half-top view as in Figure 2 with the T in position. Divide the T in Figure 1 into equal spaces as 1 to 5, and draw a line from each point to intersect the slant line A–C. Draw a line from the intersecting points 1 to 5 on line A–C in Figure 1 to intersect line G–D' in Figure 2. Use point A' as a center to draw the arcs from the intersecting points on line G–D' to intersect line F. Draw a line from point A' through each point $1'$ to $5'$ on line F to intersect the large half circle G–B', represented by points $1''$ to $5''$.

To lay out the T pattern as in Figure 3, draw line D'–D' equal to the perimeter of the T in Figure 1 and the spaces $1F$ to $5F$. Transfer the lengths on line F to $1'$, $2'$, $3'$, $4'$, and $5'$ in Figure 2 to their respective lines in Figure 3. Transfer the distance D' to A' from Figure 2 to their respective lines in Figure 3, and draw the arcs E to 5 and $1'$ to $1'$ and the freehand curves 1 to 5.

Use the distance A to C in Figure 1 as a radius to draw the arc C to C in Figure 4. Use the distances from A to points 1, 2, 3, 4, and 5 on line A–C in Figure 1 as radius lengths to draw the arcs 1–5 at line A–C in Figure 4. Transfer the spaces from point B' to $1''$ on the half circle G–B' in Figure 2, to arc C–C in Figure 4. Draw a line from each point on arc C–C to point A, crossing their respective arcs to obtain the freehand curves 1 to 5.

PLATE 113

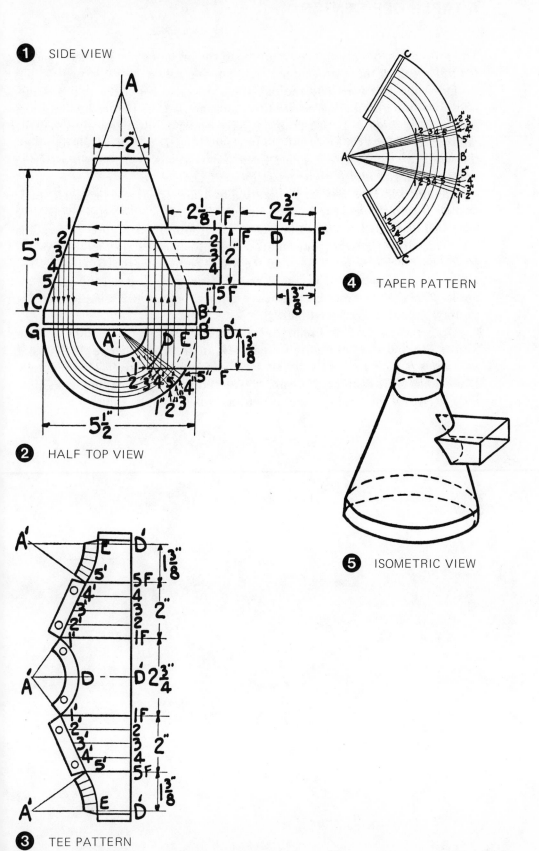

① SIDE VIEW

② HALF TOP VIEW

③ TEE PATTERN

④ TAPER PATTERN

⑤ ISOMETRIC VIEW

PLATE 114   RECTANGULAR HORIZONTAL T ON

A TAPER OFF CENTER

The procedure for this plate is identical to the previous plate, except placing the full width of the T off center in the half-top view.

Draw the side view and the half-top view as in Figures 1 and 2. Draw lines from the intersecting points 1 to 5 on line $A-C$ in Figure 1 to intersect line $F-B'$ in Figure 2. Use point A' as a center to draw an arc from the intersecting points on line $F-B'$, to intersect lines D and E which represent the width of the T. Draw a line from point A' through each intersecting point on lines D and E to intersect the half circle $F-B'$.

Lay out the T pattern as in Figure 3 by transferring the lengths $1'$ to $5'$ on line D and the lengths $1''$ to $5''$ on line E in Figure 2 to their respective lines in Figure 3. Use the distances A' to $5'$ and $5''$ in Figure 2 as radius lengths to draw the arcs from points $5'$ to $5''$ to cross each other at point A, obtaining the center point to draw the arc $5'$ to $5''$ in Figure 3. Use the distances A' to $1'$ and $1''$ in Figure 2 as radius lengths to draw the arcs from points $1'$ and $1''$ to cross each other at points A' to obtain the center point to draw the arc $1'$ to $1''$ in Figure 3.

Draw the arc $C-C$ in Figure 4; transfer the spaces 1 to 5 on line $A-C$ in Figure 2 to line $A-C$ in Figure 4, and draw an arc from each point. Transfer the spaces B' to $1''$ on the half circle $F-B'$ in Figure 2 to arc $C-C$ in Figure 4. Draw a line from each point on arc $C-C$ to point A, crossing their respective lines to obtain the freehand curve $1''$ to $5''$ and $1'$ to $5'$ as shown.

PLATE 114

1 SIDE VIEW

2 HALF TOP VIEW

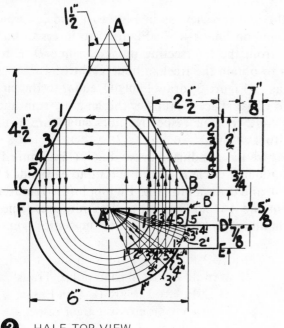

4 TAPER PATTERN

OUTSIDE

3 TEE PATTERN

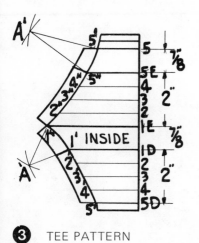

INSIDE

5 ISOMETRIC VIEW

PLATE 115   ROUND HORIZONTAL T ON A TAPER

The procedure for this plate is similar to the method used for the rectangular T's in previous plates.

Draw the side view and the half-top view as in Figures 1 and 2. Draw lines from the intersecting points on line $A-C$ in Figure 1 to intersect line $D-E$ in Figure 2. Draw arcs from the intersecting points on line $D-E$ to intersect their respective lines to obtain the freehand curve 1' to 5'.

To lay out the T pattern as in Figure 3, draw line 1–1 equal to the circumference, and divide it into equal spaces. Transfer the lengths from line F–4 to points 1' to 7' in Figure 2 to their respective lines in Figure 3, to obtain the freehand curve 1' to 1'.

Use the distance $A-C$ in Figure 1 as a radius to draw arc $C-C$ in Figure 4. Transfer the spaces E to 5" on the half circle $E-D$ in Figure 2 to each side of point E on arc $C-C$ in Figure 4, and draw a line from each point A. Transfer the lengths 1 to 7 from the slant line $A-C$ in Figure 1 to their respective lines in Figure 4 to obtain the freehand curve 1 to 7.

PLATE 115

① SIDE VIEW

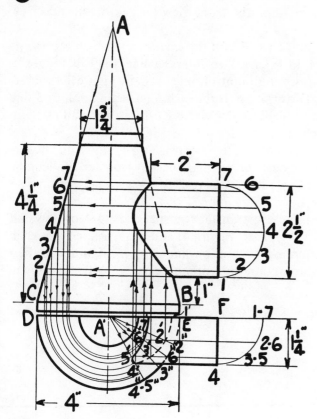

② HALF TOP VIEW

③ TEE PATTERN

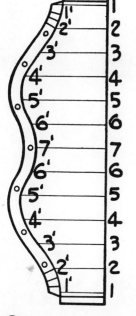

④ TAPER PATTERN

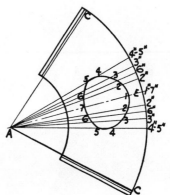

⑤ ISOMETRIC VIEW

199

PLATE 116   ROUND HORIZONTAL T ON A TAPER OFF CENTER

The procedure for this plate is similar to the method used in the previous plate. In order to simplify matters, the front view instead of the side view is drawn in Figure 1.

Draw a line from each point 1 to 12 on the small circle which represents the circumference of the T in Figure 1 to intersect line 4–10 in Figure 2. Draw a line from each intersecting point on line *A–C* in Figure 1 to intersect line *D–E* in Figure 2. Draw an arc from each intersecting point on line *D–E* to intersect their respective lines drawn down from the small circle in Figure 1 to obtain the freehand curve 1″ to 12″.

To lay out the T pattern as in Figure 3, draw line 7–7 equal to the circumference of the T, and divide it into equal spaces. Transfer the lengths from line 4–10 to points 1″ to 12″ in Figure 2 to their respective lines in Figure 3, to obtain the freehand curve 7″ to 7″.

Draw the arc *C–C* in Figure 4, transfer the spaces *E* to 4 on the half circle *D–E* in Figure 2 to arc *C–C* in Figure 4, and draw a line from each to point *A*. Transfer the lengths 1′–7′–12′ on line *A–C* in Figure 1 to their respective lines in Figure 4, to obtain the freehand curve 1′ to 12′, as shown.

PLATE 116

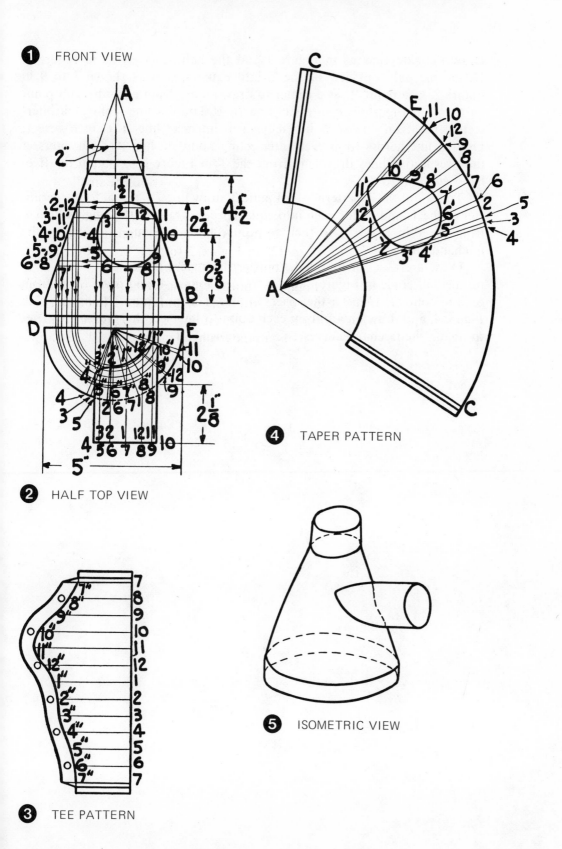

1 FRONT VIEW

2 HALF TOP VIEW

3 TEE PATTERN

4 TAPER PATTERN

5 ISOMETRIC VIEW

PLATE 117 **RECTANGULAR T VERTICALLY ON A TAPER**

Draw the side view as in Figure 1 and the half-top view as in Figure 2. Divide the half-top view of the T into equal spaces as shown 1 to 9 in Figure 2. Use point A' as a center to draw an arc from each division point on the T in Figure 2 to intersect line $D-E$. Draw a line from each intersecting point on line $D-E$ in Figure 2 to intersect line $A-C$ in Figure 1. Draw a line across from each intersecting point on line $A-C$ to intersect their respective lines drawn up from the T in Figure 2 to obtain the freehand curve $3'$ to $7'$.

To lay out the T pattern as in Figure 3, draw line 7–7 equal to the perimeter of the T, and divide each into equal spaces. Transfer the heights $1'$ to $9'$ from the T in Figure 1 to their respective lines in Figure 3 to obtain the freehand curves.

Draw arc $C-C$ in Figure 4, transfer the spaces from point $1''-9''$ to $7''$ on the half circle in Figure 2 to arc $C-C$ in Figure 4, and draw a line from each to point A. Transfer the spaces on line $A-C$ in Figure 1 to line $A-C$ in Figure 4, and draw an arc from each point to intersect their respective lines to obtain the freehand curves 1 to 9 as shown.

PLATE 117

1 SIDE VIEW

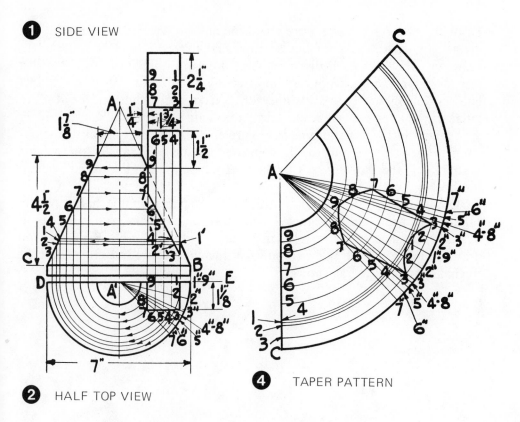

2 HALF TOP VIEW

4 TAPER PATTERN

3 TEE PATTERN

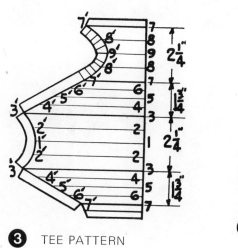

5 ISOMETRIC VIEW

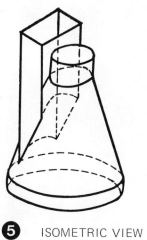

PLATE 118   ROUND T VERTICALLY ON A TAPER

Draw the side view as in Figure 1 and the half-top view as in Figure 2, and divide the half-top view of the T into equal spaces. Use A' as a center to draw an   arc from each division point on the T in Figure 2 to intersect line $D-E$. Draw a line from each intersecting point on line $D-E$ to intersect line $A-C$ in Figure 1. Draw a line across from each point on line $A-C$ to intersect their respective lines on the T to obtain the freehand curve 1' to 7'.

To lay out the T pattern as in Figure 3, draw line 1–1 equal to the circumference of the T and divide it into equal spaces. Transfer the heights 1' to 7' from the T in Figure 1 to their respective lines in Figure 3 to obtain the freehand curve 1' to 7'.

Draw arc $C-C$ in Figure 4, transfer the spaces on the half circle in Figure 2 to arc $C-C$ in Figure 4, and draw a line from each point to A. Transfer the spaces on line $A-C$ in Figure 1 to line $A-C$ in Figure 4, and draw an arc from each point to intersect their respective lines to obtain the freehand curve 1 to 7 as shown.

PLATE 118

1 SIDE VIEW

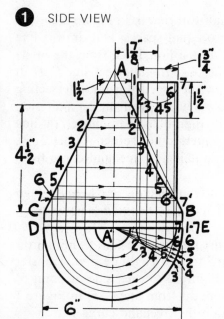

2 HALF TOP VIEW

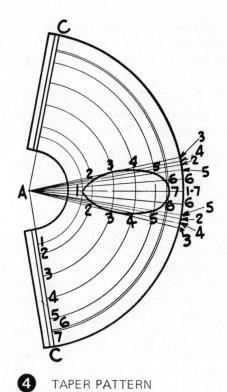

4 TAPER PATTERN

3 TEE PATTERN

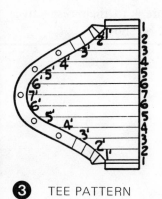

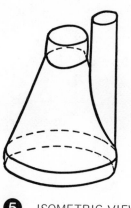

5 ISOMETRIC VIEW

PLATE 119 VERTICAL TAPERING T ON A LARGER TAPER

Draw the side view as in Figure 1 and the half-top view as in Figure 2. Divide the slant line *C–5′* from point 1′ to 5′ into equal spaces, and draw a line across each point to intersect line *A–B*. Draw a line down from the intersecting points of lines 2, 3, and 4 on line *A–B* to intersect line *E–D* in Figure 2. Use point *A′* as a center to draw the arcs from the intersecting points of lines 2, 3, and 4 on line *E–D*. Draw a line down from each division point on line *C–5′* to intersect line *E–D* in Figure 2. Use point *C′* on line *E–D* as a center to draw the arcs from the intersecting points of lines 2′, 3′, and 4′ to intersect their respective arcs to obtain the freehand curve from 1″ to 5″.

Draw straight lines from the center point *C* in Figure 2, crossing through points 2′, 3′, and 4′ to intersect the small half circle, obtaining points 2″, 3″, and 4″.

To lay out the T pattern as in Figure 3, use the distance *C* to 5′ in Figure 1 as a radius to draw the arc 1″–1″ in Figure 3 to any length desired. Transfer the spaces 5″ to 1″ on the curved line in Figure 2 to each side of point 5″ to 1″ on the arc in Figure 3. Transfer the lengths from line *C–5′* in Figure 1 to their respective lines in Figure 3 to obtain the freehand curve 1′ to 5′.

Draw straight lines from point *A′* in Figure 2, through point 2′, 3′, and 4′ to intersect the large half circle, obtaining points 2–3 and 4.

Draw arc *B–B* in Figure 4, transfer the spaces 1–5 to 2–3 on the half circle in Figure 2 to arc *B–B* in Figure 4, and draw a line from each to point *A*. Transfer the lengths on line *A–B* in Figure 1 to their respective lines in Figure 4 to obtain the freehand curve 1 to 5 as shown.

PLATE 119

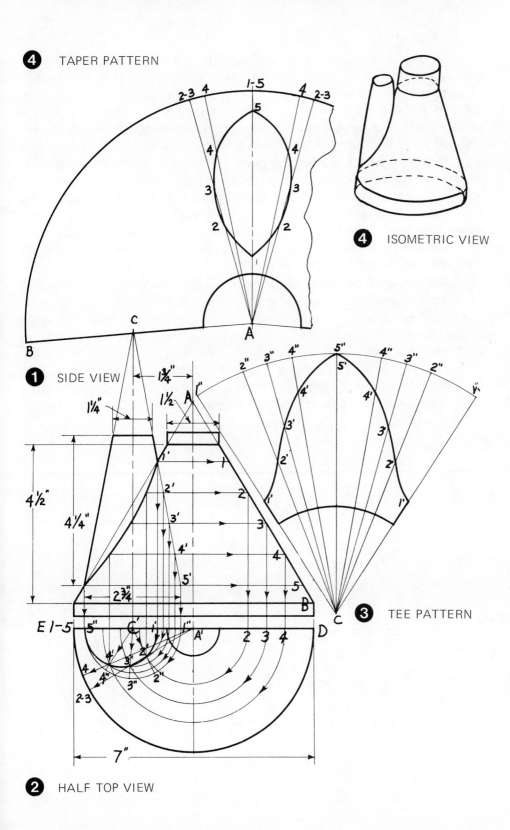

4 TAPER PATTERN

4 ISOMETRIC VIEW

1 SIDE VIEW

1¾"

1¼"

1½"

4½"

4¼"

2¾"

3 TEE PATTERN

E 1-5

7"

2 HALF TOP VIEW

PLATE 120   HORIZONTAL TAPERING T ON A LARGER TAPER

Draw the side view as in Figure 1 and the top view as in Figure 2. Draw the half circle 1 to 7 in Figure 1 and the quarter circle 1–7 to 4 in Figure 2. Divide each into equal spaces, and draw a straight line from each division point to intersect the center line A. Draw a slant line from each intersecting point on line A to point D. From the intersecting points on line $A–B$, represented by 2″ to 6″, draw a straight line across to intersect line $A–C$. Draw a line down from each intersecting point on line $A–C$ to intersect line $E–D$ in Figure 2. Use A' as a center to draw an arc from each intersecting point on line $E–D$ to intersect their respective lines to obtain the freehand curve 1 to 7. Draw a line up from each point on the freehand curved line in Figure 2, to intersect line 7–D in Figure 2. (By drawing the lines down from each point 1 to 7 on the freehand curve line in Fig. 2, to intersect line 4–D in Fig. 2, the same results may be obtained.)

To lay out the T pattern as in Figure 3, use the distance D to 7 in Figure 1 (or D to 4 in Fig. 2) as a radius to draw the arc 7–7 in Figure 3 equal to twice the number of spaces on the half circle in Figure 1. Transfer the lengths on the slant line D–7 in Figure 1 to their respective lines in Figure 3 to obtain the freehand curve 7′ to 7′.

To lay out the T opening as in Figure 4, transfer the spaces 1–7 to 3 on the large half circle in Figure 2 to line $B–B$ in Figure 4. Transfer the lengths 1″ to 7′ on line $A–B$ in Figure 1 to their respective lines in Figure 4 to obtain the freehand curve 1″ to 7″ as shown.

PLATE 120

1 SIDE VIEW

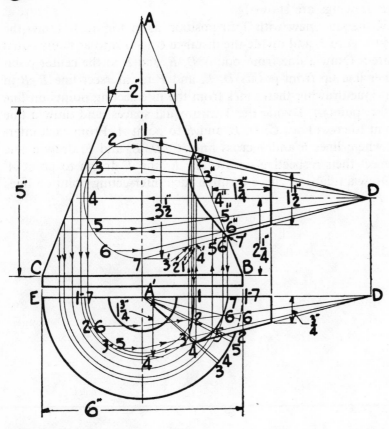

2 HALF TOP VIEW

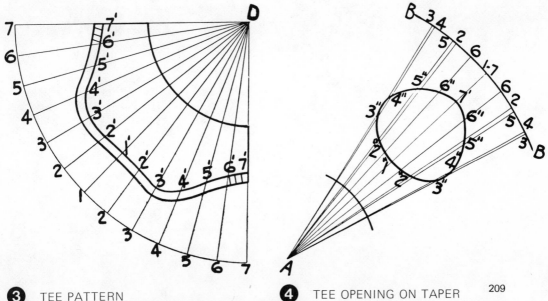

3 TEE PATTERN

4 TEE OPENING ON TAPER

PLATE 121   RECTANGULAR T INTERSECTING A

TAPER AT 45 DEG.

In order to clarify the procedure for obtaining a 45-deg. T intersection, a series of three drawings are shown.

First, draw the side view with T in position as in Figure 1. Draw the half circle as in Figure 2, and divide the distance C to G into as many equal spaces as desired. Draw a line from points D, E, and F to the center point A', and another line up from points D, E, and F to intersect line B–B in Figure 1. Continue drawing these lines from the intersecting points on line B–B to intersect point A. Divide the T into equal spaces, and draw a line from each point to cross lines C, D, E, and F to point A. From each intersecting point where lines 6 and 7 cross lines C, D, E, and F, draw a line down to intersect their respective lines C, D, E, and F drawn to point A' in Figure 2. Draw a freehand curve through each intersecting point on lines C, D, E, and F.

PLATE 121

1 SIDE VIEW

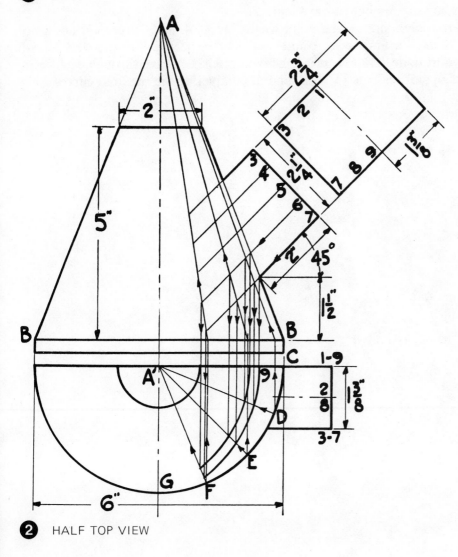

2 HALF TOP VIEW

PLATE 122   RECTANGULAR T INTERSECTING A TAPER AT 45 DEG.

This plate is a continuation of Plate 121 to show how the remaining free-hand curves are obtained in Figure 2.

From each intersecting point where lines 3, 4, and 5 cross lines C, D, E, and F, draw a line down to intersect their respective lines C, D, E, and F drawn to point A' in Figure 2. Draw a freehand curve through each intersecting point on lines C, D, E, and F, completing the required curves.

PLATE 122

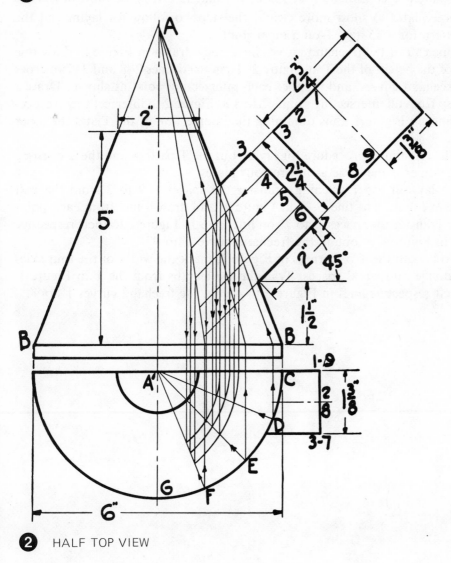

① SIDE VIEW

② HALF TOP VIEW

PLATE 123   **RECTANGULAR T INTERSECTING A TAPER AT 45 DEG.**

This plate is a continuation of Plates 121 and 122. It is the third in a series of three plates to show more clearly the steps to follow for laying out the T pattern for a 45-deg. T on a taper joint.

Since all of the freehand curves have been drawn in Figure 2, draw one half of the height of the T at Figure 2. Then draw lines 2–8 and 3–7 to cross the freehand curves, and number each intersecting point as shown. Draw a line up from all intersecting points 2 to 8 in Figure 2 to intersect their respective lines in Figure 1, thus obtaining the intersection of the T and the taper joint.

The remaining procedure for laying out the T pattern and the T opening on the taper is the same as in previous plates.

To lay out the T opening, transfer the spaces 1–9 to 3 from the half circle in Figure 2 to line B–B in Figure 4, and draw a line from each point to A. Transfer the spaces 1′ to 7″ on line A–B in Figure 1 to their respective lines in Figure 4 to obtain the freehand curve 1′ to 9′.

To lay out the T pattern as in Figure 3, mark the width of the four sides and divide into equal spaces. Transfer the lengths from the T in Figure 1, to their respective lines in Figure 3 to obtain the freehand curves 1′ to 9′.

PLATE 123

1 SIDE VIEW

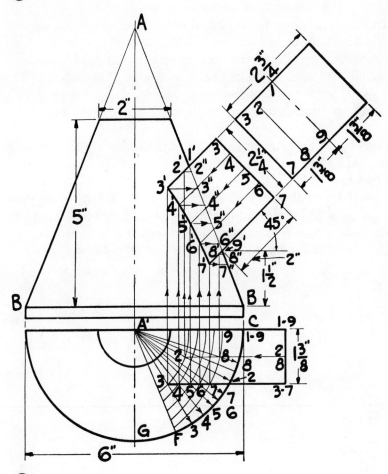

2 HALF TOP VIEW

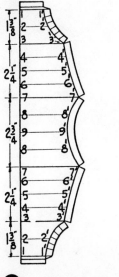

3 TEE PATTERN

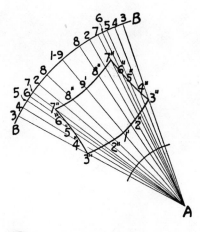

4 TEE OPENING ON TAPER

PLATE 124 **RECTANGULAR 45-DEG. T INTERSECTING
A TAPER OFF CENTER**

The procedure for this plate is the same as for previous Plates 121, 122, and 123, except that the T in Figure 2 is drawn off center.

Draw the freehand curves in Figure 2 and the T off center to the dimensions as shown. Draw lines 1–9, 2–8, and 3–7 to cross the freehand curves, and number the points 1 to 12. Draw a line up from points 3, 4, 5, 6, and 7 in Figure 2 to intersect their respective lines in Figure 1 to represent the intersection of the T on one side of the taper. Draw a line up from points 9, 10, 11, 12, and 1 to represent the intersection of the T on the other side of the taper.

To lay out the T pattern as in Figure 3, mark the width of the four sides and divide into equal spaces. Transfer the lengths from the T in Figure 1 to their respective lines in Figure 3.

To lay out the T opening as in Figure 4, transfer the spaces from point C to 3 on the half circle in Figure 2 to line B–B in Figure 4, and draw a line from each point to A. Transfer the spaces 1″ to 7″ on line A–B in Figure 1 to their respective lines in Figure 4 to obtain the freehand curve 1″ to 12″.

PLATE 124

1 SIDE VIEW

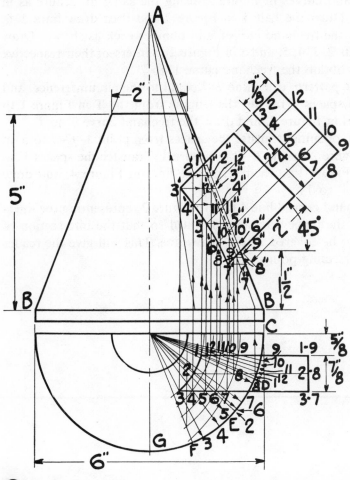

2 HALF TOP VIEW

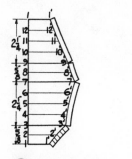

3 TEE PATTERN

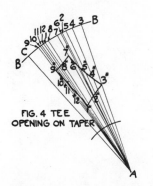

FIG. 4 TEE
OPENING ON TAPER

4 TEE OPENING ON TAPER

PLATE 125   **ROUND T INTERSECTING A TAPER AT 45 DEG.**

The procedure for this plate is the same as for Plates 121, 122, and 123.

Draw the freehand curves in Figure 2, using the same procedure as in the previous plate. Draw the half T in Figure 2 and then draw lines 2–6, 3–5, and 4 to cross the freehand curves, and number each as shown. Draw a line up from points 2, 3, 4, 5, and 6 in Figure 2 to intersect their respective lines in Figure 1 to obtain the freehand curve 1′ to 7′.

To lay out the T pattern, draw line 7–7 equal to the circumference, and divide it into equal spaces. Transfer the lengths from the T in Figure 1 to their respective lines in Figure 3, and draw the freehand curve 7′ to 7′.

To lay out the T opening, transfer the spaces from point 1–C–7 to 5 on the half circle in Figure 2 to line B–B in Figure 4. Transfer the spaces 1′ to 7′ on line A–B in Figure 1 to their respective lines in Figure 4, and draw the freehand curve 1′ to 7′.

NOTE: The freehand curved line 4 to 7 in Figure 2 representing the intersection of the T to the taper was not continued so that the intersection of those points will not be covered with a heavy line. This will give the reader a clear view of intersecting points.

PLATE 125

1 SIDE VIEW

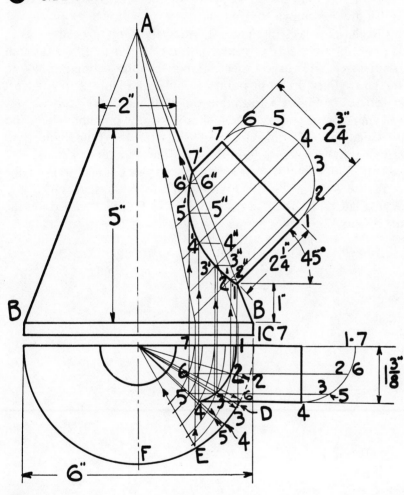

2 HALF TOP VIEW

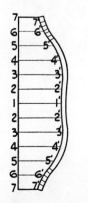

3 TEE PATTERN

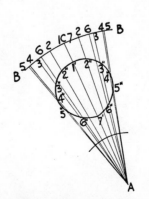

4 TEE OPENING ON TAPER

PLATE 126   ROUND 45-DEG. T INTERSECTING
A TAPER OFF CENTER

The procedure for this plate is the same as for the previous plate, except that the T in Figure 2 is drawn off center.

Draw the freehand curves in Figure 2, using the same procedure as in the previous plate. Draw the T off center and the lines 4 to 10 on the half circle to cross the freehand curves; then number the intersecting points 1 to 12 as shown. Draw lines up from points 1 to 12 in Figure 2 to intersect their respective lines in Figure 1 to obtain the freehand curve 1' to 12'.

To lay out the T pattern, draw line 4–4 equal to the circumference, and divide it into equal spaces. Transfer the lengths from the T in Figure 1 to their respective lines in Figure 3, and draw the freehand curve 4' to 4'.

To lay out the T opening, transfer the spaces from point C to 9 on the half circle in Figure 2 to line $B-B$ in Figure 4. Transfer the spaces 6″ to 12″ on line $A-B$ in Figure 1 to their respective lines in Figure 4, and draw the freehand curve 1″ to 12″.

PLATE 126

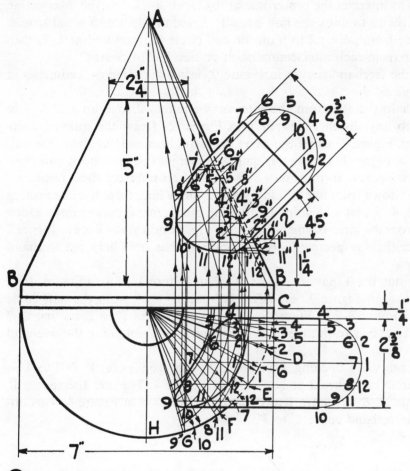

1 SIDE VIEW

2 HALF TOP VIEW

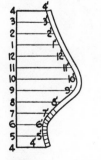

3 TEE PATTERN

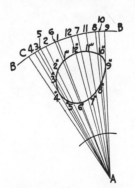

4 TEE OPENING ON TAPER

PLATE 127   ROUND TAPERING T INTERSECTING

A TAPER AT 45 DEG.

To obtain the T to intersect the taper as in Figure 1, draw the center line of the T *C*–4 to intersect the center line of the taper *A*–*H*. Use the intersecting point as a center to draw the half circle 1–7, and divide it into equal spaces. Draw a line from points 2 to 6 on the half circle to intersect line 1–7, then draw a line from each intersecting point on line 1–7 to point *C*.

Draw the freehand curves in Figure 2, using the same procedure as in previous plates.

Draw a line down from the intersecting points 2 to 6 on line 1–7 in Figure 1 to any distance desired into Figure 2. Draw the quarter circle 1–7 to 4 in Figure 2, using the same radius as was used to draw the half circle 1–7 in Figure 1. Divide this quarter circle into equal spaces, and draw straight lines across from points 2–6 and 3–5 to intersect their respective lines drawn down from line 1–7 in Figure 1. Draw lines from the intersecting points 2, 3, 4, 5, and 6 to point *D*, crossing the freehand curved lines. Draw a line up from the intersecting points on the freehand curved lines in Figure 2 to intersect their respective lines in Figure 1, thus obtaining the freehand curve 1″ to 7′.

To lay out the T pattern, use *C* to 7 in Figure 1 as a radius to draw the arc 7 to 7 in Figure 3. Transfer the spaces 1 to 7 from the half circle in Figure 1 to arc 7–7 in Figure 3. Transfer the spaces 7′ to 2′ on line *C*–7 in Figure 1 to their respective lines in Figure 3, thus obtaining the freehand curve 7′ to 7′.

To lay out the T opening, transfer the spaces from point 1–*E*–7 to 4 on the half circle in Figure 2 to line *B*–*B* in Figure 4. Transfer the spaces 1″ to 7′ on line *A*–*B* in Figure 1 to their respective lines in Figure 4, thus obtaining the freehand curve 1″ to 7′.

PLATE 127

1 SIDE VIEW

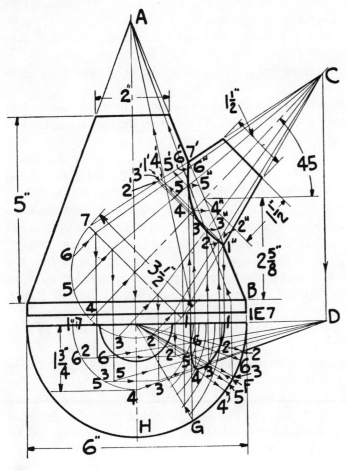

2 HALF TOP VIEW

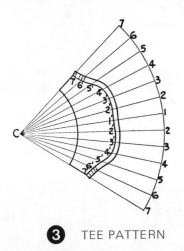

3 TEE PATTERN

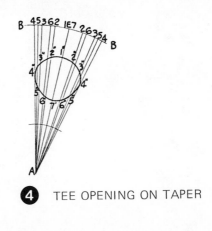

4 TEE OPENING ON TAPER

PLATE 128 **ROUND TAPERING T INTERSECTING**

A TAPER AT 45 DEG.

To draw the T to intersect the taper as in Figure 1, draw the center line
C–4 to intersect the center A–H. Draw the half circle 1–7, and divide it
into equal spaces. Draw a line from points 2 to 6 on the half circle to intersect line 1–7; then draw a line from each intersecting point on line 1–7 to
point C.

Draw the freehand curves in Figure 2, using the same procedure as in
previous plates.

Draw a line down from the intersecting points 2 to 6 on line 1–7 in
Figure 1 to any distance desired into Figure 2. Draw the quarter circle 1–7
to 4 in Figure 2, using the same radius as was used to draw the half circle
1–7 in Figure 1. Divide it into equal spaces, and draw a straight line across
from points 2–6, 3–5, and 4 to intersect their respective lines drawn down
from line 1–7 in Figure 1. Draw lines from the intersecting points 2, 3, 4,
5, and 6 to point D crossing the freehand curved lines. Draw lines up from
the intersecting points on the freehand curved lines in Figure 2 to intersect
their respective lines in Figure 1, thus obtaining the freehand curve 1′ to 7″.

To lay out the T pattern, use C to 7 in Figure 1 as a radius to draw the
arc 7 to 7 in Figure 3. Transfer the spaces 1 to 7 from the half circle in
Figure 1 to arc 7–7 in Figure 3. Transfer the spaces 1′ to 7′ on line C–1 in
Figure 1 to their respective lines in Figure 3.

To lay out the T opening, transfer the spaces from point 1–E–7 to 3 on
the half circle in Figure 2 to line B–B in Figure 4. Transfer the spaces 1′ to
7″ on line A–B in Figure 1 to their respective lines in Figure 4, thus obtaining the freehand curve 1″ to 7″.

NOTE: The freehand curved line 4 to 1 in Figure 2 representing the half
top view of the tapering T was not continued so that the intersection of
those points will not be covered with a heavy line. This will give the reader
a clear view of intersecting points.

PLATE 128

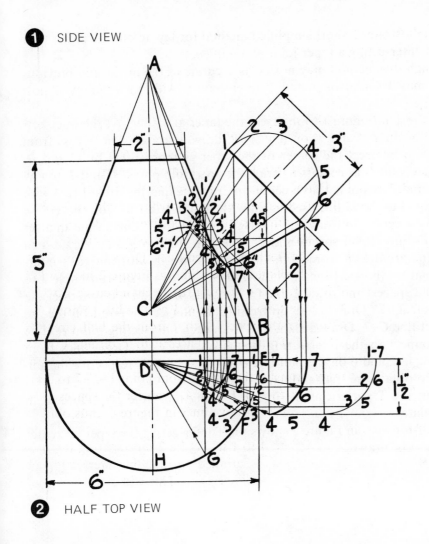

1 SIDE VIEW

2 HALF TOP VIEW

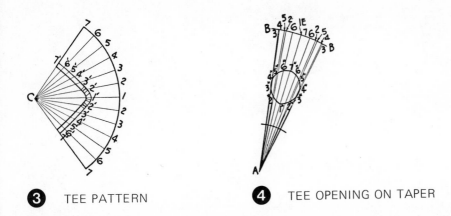

3 TEE PATTERN

4 TEE OPENING ON TAPER

PLATE 129   SHORT METHOD: ROUND T INTERSECTING

A TAPER AT 45 DEG.

This plate illustrates a short simplified method for laying out the pattern for a round T intersecting a taper joint at an angle.

Although this method may not be as accurate as the method in previous plates, it may be used on many T intersections with an accuracy almost foolproof.

Draw the T in Figure 1 to intersect the taper at 45 deg. At the intersecting points of lines 1' and 7' on line A–B, draw a straight line across from each point to intersect the center of the taper as represented by C and D. Use points C and D as centers to draw the arcs from points 1' and 7' to any length desired. Use point 1' as a center to draw the quarter circle 1 to 4 with a radius equal to the radius used to draw the half circle 1 to 7 on the T. Use point 7' as a center to draw the quarter circle 4 to 7. Divide the quarter circle 1 to 4 into equal spaces and draw a line from points 2, 3, and 4 to intersect the arc drawn from point 1'. Draw a line down from each intersecting point on the arc to intersect line D–1. Divide the quarter circle 4 to 7 into equal spaces, and draw a line from points 4, 5, and 6 to intersect the arc drawn from 7'. Draw a line up from each intersecting point on the arc to intersect line C–7. Draw a slant line from each intersecting point on line D–1 to connect to the intersecting points on line C–7. Draw lines from points 2, 3, 4, 5, and 6 on the half circle to intersect their respective lines in the taper to obtain the freehand curve 1' to 7'.

Lay out the T pattern as in Figure 3, using the same procedure as in previous plates.

The half-top view in Figure 2 shows the T intersecting the taper on center and need not be drawn.

PLATE 129

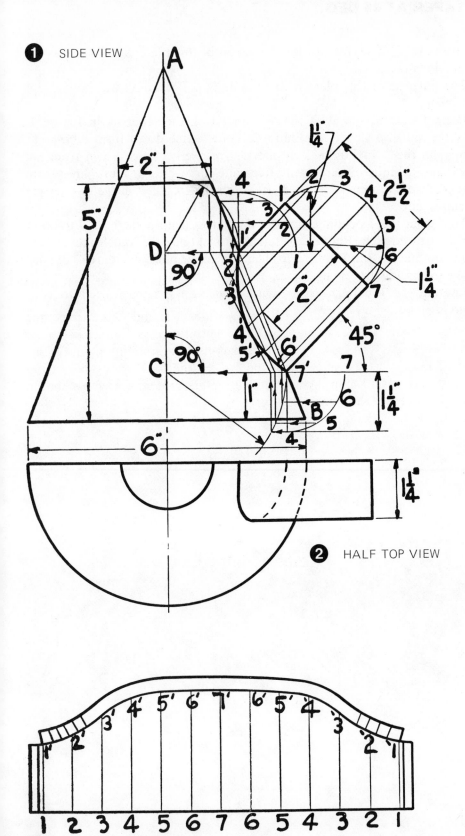

1 SIDE VIEW

2 HALF TOP VIEW

3 TEE PATTERN

227

PLATE 130   SHORT METHOD: ROUND T INTERSECTING

A TAPER AT 45 DEG.

The procedure for laying out the T pattern in this plate is the same as for the previous plate.

The purpose of this plate is to show how a T opening can be laid out on a taper.

Draw the side view with the T intersecting the taper as in Figure 1. Draw the half-top view as in Figure 2. Draw a line down from each point 1' to 7' on the T in Figure 1 to intersect respective lines drawn from the T in Figure 2, thus obtaining the freehand curve 1 to 7. Draw lines from point A' through points 2, 3, 4, 5, and 6 on the freehand curve to intersect the half circle.

To lay out the T opening, transfer the spaces from point $1-E-7$ to point 4 on the half circle in Figure 2 to line $B-B$ in Figure 4. Transfer the spaces 1' to 7' on line $A-B$ in Figure 1 to their respective lines in Figure 4, obtaining the freehand curve 1' to 7'.

Lay out the T pattern as in Figure 3, using the same procedure as in previous plates.

PLATE 130

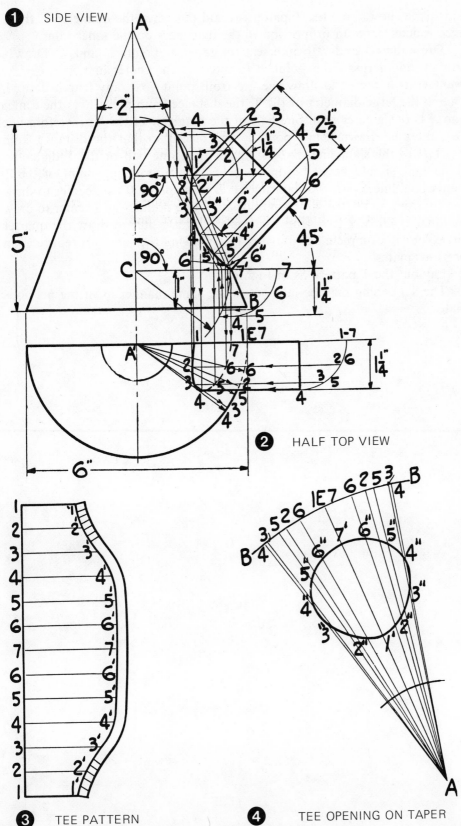

1 SIDE VIEW

A

2"

5"

D

90°

C

90°

B

45°

2½"

1¼"

1¼"

6"

2 HALF TOP VIEW

1¼"

3 TEE PATTERN

4 TEE OPENING ON TAPER

229

PLATE 131 **SHORT METHOD: LARGE ROUND T INTERSECTING A TAPER AT 45 DEG.**

This plate shows how the T pattern is laid out when the diameter of the T is considered large in proportion to the diameters on the taper joint.

Draw lines 1 and 7 to intersect the taper at points 1′ and 7′. Draw a straight line across from point 7′ to intersect the center line A at C. Use point C as a center to draw the arc from point 7′ to any length desired. Due to the large diameter of the T, the distance from point 1′ to the center line A is not greater than one half of the diameter of the T; therefore line D–1 must be drawn below point 1′ and placed so that the distance from point D to the slant line A–B is greater than one half of the T diameter. (Line D–1 should never be drawn below the intersecting point of the T center line, line 4, nor the slant line A–B.) Use point D as a center to draw the arc from point 1″ to any length desired. Use point 1″ as a center to draw the quarter circle 1 to 4, and use point 7′ as a center to draw the quarter circle 4 to 7. Complete the drawing by following the same procedure as in previous plates.

Lay out the T pattern as in Figure 2.

The T opening may be laid out in the same manner as in the previous plate.

PLATE 131

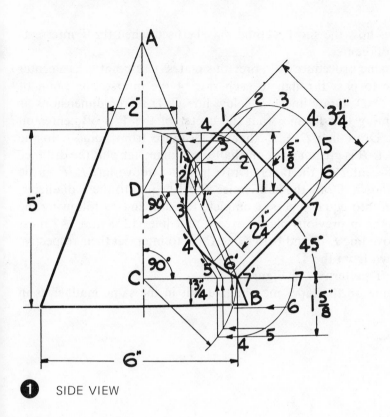

1 SIDE VIEW

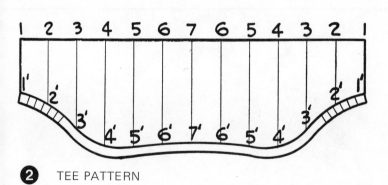

2 TEE PATTERN

231

PLATE 132 **SHORT METHOD: ROUND 45-DEG. T INTERSECTING A TAPER OFF CENTER**

This plate shows how the short method may be used when the T intersects the taper joint off center.

Follow the same procedure as in previous plates. Use point *C* as a center to draw the arc to pass through to each side of the intersecting point of lines *A–B* and *C–D*. Draw line 1–7 below line *C–D* to the dimensions as shown, representing the distance that the center of the T is off center on the taper joint. Draw line *E–F* so that the distance from point *E* to the crossing of line *A–B* is greater than one half the T diameter plus the distance that the T is off center on the taper. Draw line 7–1 above line *E–F* to the dimensions as shown. Draw the half circles 4 to 10 equal to the T diameter, and divide them into equal spaces. Complete the drawing by following the same procedure as in previous plates, except that lines 12–8 and 1–7 must be extended above line *E–F* and below line *C–D* to intersect their respective lines drawn down from the T.

Lay out the T pattern as in Figure 2.

The T opening on the taper may be laid out in the same manner as in previous plates.

PLATE 132

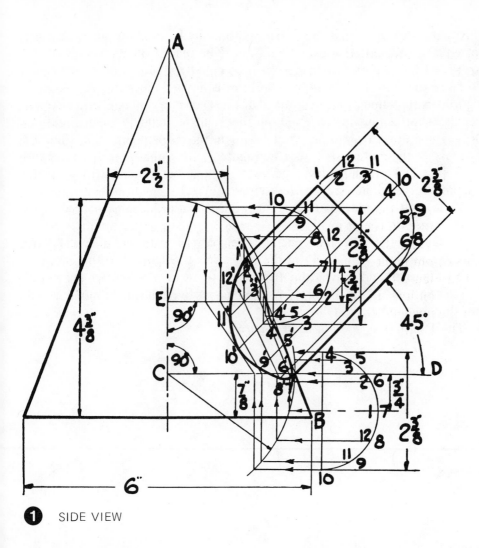

1 SIDE VIEW

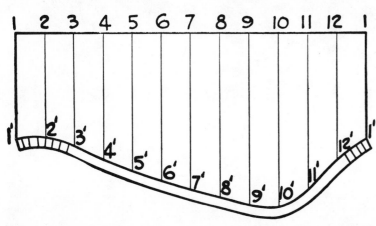

2 TEE PATTERN

This plate is to show that the short method may be used on tapers that are not equally tapered. However, the T must be placed on the center of the taper, and the two opposite sides must be equally tapered.

The procedure for obtaining the intersection of the T on the taper in Figure 1 is the same as in previous plates, except that points C and D intersect the slant center line $A-B$. Draw the T in the half-top view, Figure 2. Draw a line down from each point 1 to 7 on the freehand curve in Figure 1 to intersect their respective lines in Figure 2, thus obtaining the freehand curve 1 to 7. Draw lines from point A through each point 2 to 6 on the freehand curve to intersect the half circle.

To lay out the taper pattern as in Figure 4, use the same procedure as for the taper off center in Plate 84.

To lay out the T opening on the taper pattern in Figure 4, transfer the spaces from point $7'-1'$ to $4'$ on the half circle in Figure 2 to the base line $1-1$ in Figure 4, and draw a line from each point to A'. Transfer the spaces $1''$ to $7''$ on line $A-7$ in Figure 1 to their respective lines in Figure 4 to obtain the freehand curve $1''$ to $7''$.

The T pattern is laid out as in Figure 3.

PLATE 133

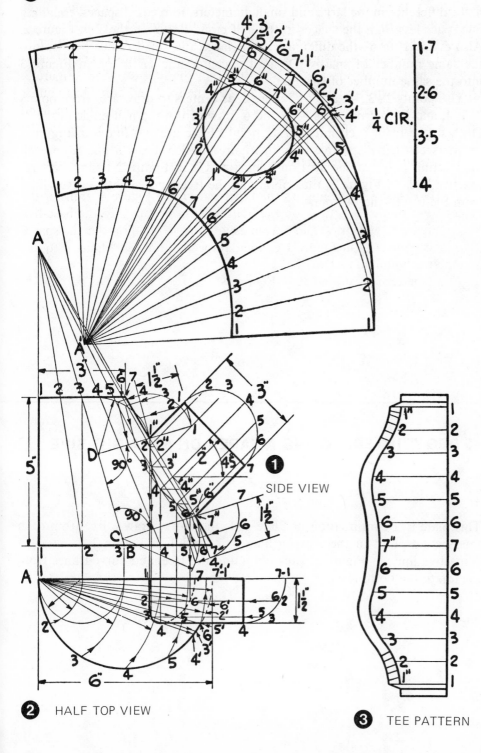

4 TAPER PATTERN

¼ CIR.

1·7

2·6

3·5

4

1 SIDE VIEW

2 HALF TOP VIEW

3 TEE PATTERN

PLATE 134   45-DEG. T INTERSECTING A TAPER ON STRAIGHT SIDE

Draw the half-top view and the side view as in Figures 2 and 3. Divide 1 to 6, the difference in the large and small diameters, into equal spaces, equalling one space less than the spaces in the half circle 1 to 7 on the T in Figure 2. Also divide 1' to 6', the difference in the large and small radius points, into the same number of spaces. Divide the center line 1E to 6F in Figure 3 into the same number of spaces.

Use points 2', 3', 4', and 5', Figure 2, as centers to draw arcs from points 2, 3, 4, and 5, to cross lines 4, 5, and 6 drawn from the half circle in the T. Draw a line from each intersecting point of the arcs on line 6 in Figure 2 to intersect their respective lines in Figure 3. Also, draw a line from each intersecting point of the arcs on lines 5 and 4 in Figure 2 to intersect respective lines in Figure 3, thus obtaining the freehand, slightly curved lines from the top to the bottom.

PLATE 135   45 DEG. T INTERSECTING A TAPER ON STRAIGHT SIDE

This plate is a continuation of Plate 134; therefore, draw a line from each intersecting point of the arcs on lines 3, 2, and 1 in Figure 2 to intersect respective lines in Figure 3, thus obtaining the freehand curved lines from the top to the bottom.

PLATE 134

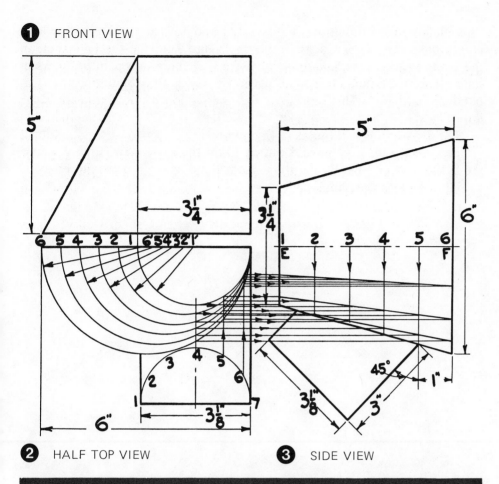

① FRONT VIEW

② HALF TOP VIEW   **③** SIDE VIEW

PLATE 135

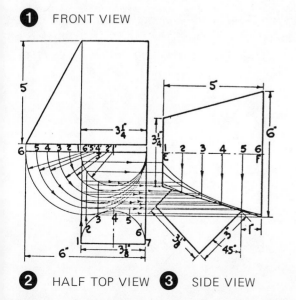

① FRONT VIEW

② HALF TOP VIEW   **③** SIDE VIEW

PLATE 136   45-DEG. T INTERSECTING A TAPER ON STRAIGHT SIDE

This plate is a continuation of plates 134 and 135. Since all the freehand curves have been drawn in the taper in Figure 3, divide the half circle in the T into equal spaces, and draw a line from each division point to intersect their respective freehand lines drawn in the taper, thus obtaining the freehand curves 1 to 7. This represents the intersection of the T and the taper joint.

The *T* pattern is laid out as in Figure 4.

The taper joint may be laid out by using the front view, Figure 1, and the half-top view, Figure 2, in the same manner as the tapers with one side straight, shown in previous plates.

PLATE 136

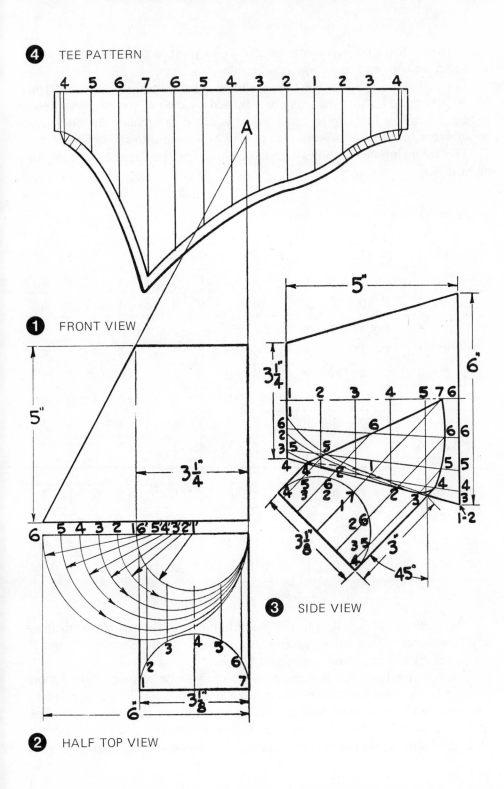

4 TEE PATTERN

1 FRONT VIEW

3 SIDE VIEW

2 HALF TOP VIEW

PLATE 137   COLLECTOR

The patterns for a collector consist of a taper joint, a cylinder, a cap with an outlet on top, and an intake on the side.

The round pipe, ·epresented by *C* shown on the inside of the collector, has a cap on the bottom that may be adjusted by the angle irons, with holes punched to allow this cap to be raised or lowered to regulate the discharge of air according to the substance that may be blown into the collector.

The following chart shows the dimensions for the various sections for eight different collectors:

	1	2	3	4	5	6	7	8
A	0′– 7″	0′–11″	1′– 1″	1′– 5″	1′– 9″	2′– 1″	2′– 5″	2′– 9″
B	1′– 0″	1′– 6″	1′– 8″	2′– 9″	2′–11″	3′–10″	4′– 1″	4′– 9″
C	1′– 2″	1′–10″	2′– 2″	2′–10″	3′– 6″	4′– 2″	4′–10″	5′– 6″
D	2′– 4″	3′– 8″	4′– 4″	5′– 8″	7′–10″	8′– 4″	9′– 8″	11′– 0″
E	1′– 9″	2′– 1″	2′– 5″	3′– 0″	3′– 7″	4′– 2″	4′– 9″	5′– 4″
F	0′– 3″	0′– 4″	0′– 5″	0′– 6″	0′– 7″	0′– 8″	0′–10″	0′–11″
G	0′– 3″	0′–3½″	0′– 4″	0′–4½″	0′– 5″	0′–5½″	0′– 6″	0′– 6″
H	2′– 2″	2′– 9″	3′– 3″	4′– 3″	5′– 3″	6′– 3″	7′– 3″	8′– 3″
I	0′– 5″	0′– 8″	0′–10″	1′– 3″	1′– 8″	2′– 1″	2′– 6″	2′–11″
J	2′– 2″	3′– 3″	3′– 9″	5′–10″	6′– 4″	7′– 6″	8′– 4″	9′–10″
K	0′– 5″	0′– 8″	0′– 9″	0′–10″	0′–10″	1′– 0″	1′– 0″	1′– 2″
L	0′–11″	1′– 5″	1′– 8″	2′– 1″	2′– 8″	3′– 2″	3′– 8″	4′– 2″
M	1′– 8″	2′– 1″	2′– 6″	3′– 1″	3′– 7″	4′– 2″	4′– 9″	5′– 4″
N	0′–3½″	0′–5½″	0′– 7″	0′–8½″	0′–10″	0′–11″	1′– 2″	1′–3½″

The method for laying out and assembling the collector is identical to any taper joint with a collar, except on a large collector. Sections *H* and *F* are joined by a companion angle-iron flange.

The top riveting edge of section *H*, which is to be connected to section *F*, must be notched and tapered in to the same angle or pitch as section *F*. This will facilitate joining sections *H* and *F* without difficulty. A feather edge that must be allowed on section *F* then is dressed down over section *H*, as shown in the elevation view, making the connection practically airtight.

PLATE 137

② TOP VIEW

FIRE DAMPER
& FUSIBLE LINK

M 24" 2"

N

AIR

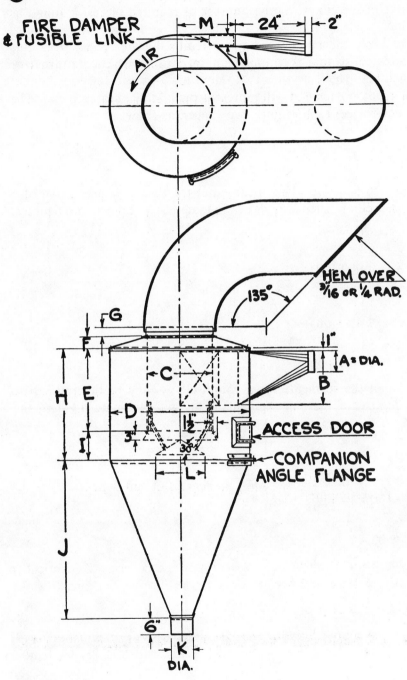

135°

HEM OVER
3/16 or 1/4 RAD.

G

F

C

A = DIA.

B

H E

D

1½"

ACCESS DOOR

3"

30°

COMPANION
ANGLE FLANGE

I

L

J

6"

K
DIA.

① ELEVATION VIEW

241

PLATE 138   FOUR-PIECE ELBOW

The width or the height of the first piece and of each remaining piece, regardless of the size of the elbow, or the number of required pieces, is found as follows:

RULE: Multiply the number of pieces required by 2. Then, from this product, subtract 2 to find the number of spaces into which the throat or heel curve will be divided.

The first space at each end will represent the first piece at each end. The remaining centerpieces each require two spaces, as shown.

SOLUTION:

For a 4-piece elbow

$4 \times 2 = 8$

$8 - 2 = 6$ divisions. This means that the throat or heel curve of a 4-piece elbow, such as is shown in Plate 128, is divided into 6 pieces.

For a 3-piece elbow

$3 \times 2 = 6$

$6 - 2 = 4$ divisions

For a 5-piece elbow

$5 \times 2 = 10$

$10 - 2 = 8$ divisions

$6 \times 2 = 12$

$12 - 2 = 10$ divisions

The height of the segments for a round elbow may be determined by finding the degrees of the end segments. This will eliminate dividing the heel curve with the dividers.

FORMULA:

$$\frac{90 \text{ deg.}}{(\text{No. of pieces required} \times 2) - 2} = \text{degrees of end segment}$$

EXAMPLE:

4-piece elbow

$$\frac{90 \text{ deg.}}{(4 \times 2) - 2} = \frac{90 \text{ deg.}}{8 - 2} = \frac{90 \text{ deg.}}{6} =$$

15 deg. for end segment

PLATE 138

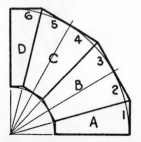

The following mathematical rule will help to obtain this distance when laying out the pattern for a frustum of a cone. It is necessary to draw only a profile to the dimensions shown and a line through the center. Knowing the distance between the base and *A* will eliminate the extra work of drawing the slant lines to find intersection at *A*.

RULE: Find the difference between the large and the small diameters. Then multiply the large diameter by the vertical height, and divide this product by the difference previously obtained. The result will be the length of the center line from the top of the cone to the intersecting point *A*.

EXAMPLE: Large diameter minus small diameter equals $10 - 6 = 4$. Vertical height $\times$ large diameter $= 12 \times 10$ in. $= 120$ in. 120 in. $\div 4 = 30$ in., which is the length of the center line.

PLATE 139

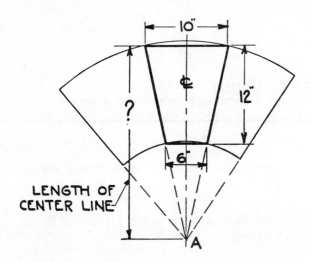

PLATE 140   FINDING CUTOUT FOR STACK CAP

RULE: To find the width of the piece to be cut out of the flat pattern shown in Figure 2, find the difference between the diameter of the base and the diameter of the flat pattern.

Then multiply this difference by 3.1416.

SOLUTION:

36 in. is the diameter of the base in Figure 1.

$2 \times 20\frac{1}{8} = 40\frac{1}{4}$ in., or the diameter of the flat pattern in Figure 2.

$40\frac{1}{4} - 36 = 4\frac{1}{4}$ in., or the difference.

$3.1416 \times 4\frac{1}{4} = 13.3518$ in. (or roughly, $13\frac{3}{8}$ in.), which is the width of the piece to be cut out.

This method can be made more efficient by using a handbook which contains the circumferences of circles. Then, by taking the circumference of a circle $4\frac{3}{8}$ in. in diameter, the dimension 13.3518 in. can be obtained very rapidly.

PLATE 141   FINDING THE DEGREE OF CUTOUT

FOR STACK CAP

RULE: To find the number of degrees in the sector to be cut out of the flat pattern in Figure 2, find the difference between the diameters of the base and of the flat pattern.

Then multiply this difference by 360, and divide the product thus obtained by the diameter of the flat pattern.

SOLUTION:

36 in. is the diameter of the base shown in Figure 1.

$40\frac{1}{4}$ in. is the diameter of the flat pattern shown in Figure 2.

$40\frac{1}{4} - 36 = 4\frac{1}{4}$ in., or the difference.

$360 \times 4\frac{1}{4} = 1530$ in.

$\dfrac{1530}{40\frac{1}{4}}$ equals 38.01, or 38 deg.

The degrees may be laid off on the pattern with a protractor.

PLATE 140

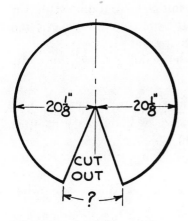

CUT OUT

? 20⅛" 20⅛"

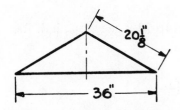

20⅛"

36"

PLATE 141

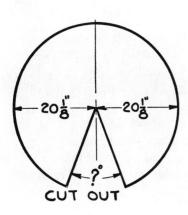

20⅛" 20⅛"

?°

CUT OUT

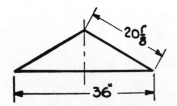

20⅛"

36"

PLATE 142 **AREA OF ELLIPSE—CIRCUMFERENCE**

OF ELLIPSE

The ellipse is closely related to the circle. If a round pipe is cut on a slant, the sectional view is a true ellipse. For this reason the sheet-metal worker often has to consider the properties of an ellipse in laying out certain patterns.

The area of an ellipse is equal to one half the major axis (A) times one half the minor axis (B), times 3.1416.

EXAMPLE: One half of the major axis (A) is equal to 20 in.; one half of the minor axis (B) is equal to 12 in. Thus, $A \times B \times 3.1416 =$ area, $20 \times 12 \times 3.1416 = 240 \times 3.1416 = 753.98$ sq. in.

The method for finding the circumference of an ellipse differs somewhat from the method for finding the area.

The circumference for an ellipse is equal to one half the major axis squared, plus one half the minor axis squared, times two; then extract the square root from the product times 3.1416.

EXAMPLE: One half of major axis (A) is equal to 20 inches, one half the minor axis (B) equals 12 inches. Thus,

$3.1416 \sqrt{2(A^2 + B^2)} =$ circumference

$3.1416 \sqrt{2(20^2 + 12^2)} = 3.1416 \sqrt{2(400 + 144)}$

$3.1416 \sqrt{2 \times 544} = 3.1416 \sqrt{1088}$

$3.1416 \times 33 = 103.67$ in. circumference.

PLATE 143 **FINDING THE LENGTH OF PIPE**

BETWEEN TWO ANGLES

Often a piece of pipe is used between two angles to represent an offset.

To find the length of the pipe between the two angles, it is necessary to calculate the distance between the two centers of the angles, as represented by C in Figure 1. This distance may be determined by multiplying the offset (A, Fig. 1) by the factor given according to the degrees of the angles. (For a 45-deg. angle, the factor is 1.414, for a 30-deg. angle, 2.00; for a 60-deg. angle, 1.154.) From the product obtained, subtract twice the distance of B, thus obtaining the length of the pipe as represented by D in Figure 1.

Distance B may be obtained by squaring in from the center of each side of one of the angles as shown in Figure 2.

EXAMPLE: The offset A in Figure 1 is 27 in.; the distance B in Figure 2 is $8\frac{1}{2}$ in.; the angles are each 45 deg., thus $A \times 1.414 - (B \times 2) = D$ (length of pipe). $27 \times 1.414 = 38.17$ in. $- (2 \times B$ in Fig. 2). $2 \times 8\frac{1}{2} = 17$ in.; $38.17 - 17 = 21.17$ or $21\frac{3}{16}$ in., which is the length of the pipe between the two 45-deg. angles, represented by D in Figure 1.

PLATE 142

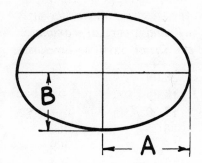

PLATE 143

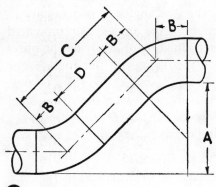

1 ASSEMBLED ANGLES

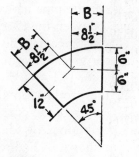

2 45° ANGLE

45° ANGLES, C = A x 1.414
30°ANGLES, C = A x 2.00
60° ANGLES, C = A x 1.154

DECIMAL EQUIVALENTS OF ONE INCH THICKNESS OF GALVANIZED IRON

No. of Gauge	Thickness Decimal	Thickness Approximate Fraction	Pounds per Sq. Ft.	Approximate Wire Thickness
7–0's	.5	$1/2$	20.00	—
6–0's	.46875	$15/32$	18.75	—
5–0's	.4375	$7/16$	17.50	—
0000	.40625	$13/32$	16.25	.460
000	.375	$3/8$	15.	.409
00	.34375	$11/32$	13.75	.365
0	.3125	$5/16$	12.5–	.325
1	.28125	$9/32$	11.25	.289
2	.265625	$17/64$	10.625	.258
3	.2391	$1/4$	10.	.229
4	.2242	$15/64$	9.375	.204
5	.2092	$7/32$	8.75	.182
6	.1943	$13/64$	8.125	.162
7	.1793	$3/16$	7.5	.144
8	.1644	$11/64$	6.875	.128
9	.1495	$5/32$	6.25	.114
10	.1345	$9/64$	5.625	.102
11	.1196	$1/8$	5.	.091
12	.1046	$7/64$	4.375	.081
13	.0897	$3/32$	3.75	.072
14	.0747	$5/64$	3.125	.064
15	.0673	$1/16$	2.8125	.057
16	.0598	$1/16$	2.5	.051
17	.0538	$3/64$	2.25	.045
18	.0478	$3/64$	2.	.040
19	.0418	$3/64$	1.75	.036
20	.0359	$1/32$	1.50	.032
21	.0329	$1/32$	1.375	.028
22	.0299	$1/32$	1.25	.025
23	.0269	$1/32$	1.125	.022
24	.0239	$1/32$	1.	.020
25	.0209	$1/64$	.875	.018
26	.0179	$1/64$	.75	.016
27	.0164	$1/64$	.6875	.014
28	.0149	$1/64$	.625	.013
29	.0135	$1/64$	.5625	.011
30	.0120	$1/64$	.5	.010
31	.01094	$1/64$	.4375	.009
32	.01016	$1/64$	.40625	.008

COMPARISON OF THICKNESS OF SHEET IRON AND COPPER

Copper Thickness			Iron or Steel Thickness		
Gauge by Wt. in Oz.	Decimal Thickness	Pounds per Sq. Ft.	Gauge U.S.S.	Decimal Thickness	Pounds per Sq. Ft.
8	.0108	$\frac{1}{2}$	31	.0109	.4375
9	.0120	$\frac{9}{16}$	30	.0120	.50
10	.0135	$\frac{5}{8}$	29	.0135	.5625
11	.0146	$\frac{11}{16}$	28	.0149	.6875
12	.0162	$\frac{3}{4}$	27	.0164	.6875
13	.0173	$\frac{13}{16}$	26	.0179	.750
14	.0189	$\frac{7}{8}$	—	—	—
15	.0202	$\frac{15}{16}$	25	.0209	.875
16	.0216	1	—	—	—
18	.0243	$1\frac{1}{8}$	24	.0239	1.
20	.0270	$1\frac{1}{4}$	23	.0269	1.125
24	.0324	$1\frac{1}{2}$	21	.0329	1.375
28	.0378	$1\frac{3}{4}$	20	.0359	1.50
32	.0432	2	19	.0418	1.75
36	.0486	$2\frac{1}{4}$	18	.0478	2.
40	.0540	$2\frac{1}{2}$	17	.0538	2.25
44	.0596	$2\frac{3}{4}$	16	.0598	2.5
48	.0648	3	15	.0673	2.8125
56	.0756	$3\frac{1}{2}$	14	.0747	3.125
64	.0864	4	13	.0897	3.75
72	.0972	$4\frac{1}{2}$	—	—	—
80	.1080	5	12	.1046	4.375
88	.1188	$5\frac{1}{2}$	11	.1196	5.
—	.1296	6	10	.1345	5.625
—	.1404	$6\frac{1}{2}$	9	.1495	6.25
—	.1512	7	9	.1495	6.25
—	.1620	$7\frac{1}{2}$	8	.1644	6.875
—	.1728	8	7	.1793	7.5

NONFERROUS METAL GAUGE

Brown and Sharpe gauge is used for measuring aluminum, brass, and all other nonferrous metals.

Gauge	Thickness	Pounds per Sq. Ft.	Gauge	Thickness	Pounds per Sq. Ft.
10	.1019	1.44	26	.0159	.225
	.1000	1.41	27	.0142	.200
	.0938	1.32	28	.0126	.178
11	.0907	1.28	29	.0113	.159
	.0900	1.27	30	.0100	.141
12	.0808	1.14			
	.0800	1.13			
	.0781	1.10			
13	.0720	1.01			
	.0703	.990		*Tin Plate*	
	.0700	.986			
14	.0641	.903	Tin Plate		Pounds per
	.0625	.880	Number	Thickness	Sq. Ft.
	.0600	.845			
15	.0571	.804	1 C	.0125	.491
	.0563	.793	1 X	.0156	.620
	.0550	.775	2 X	.0189	.711
16	.0508	.716	3 X	.0203	.804
	.0500	.704	4 X	.0150	.638
17	.0453	.638			
	.0450	.634			
	.438	.617			
18	.0403	.568			
	.0400	.563	D C	.0150	.638
	.0375	.528	D X	.0203	.827
	.0360	.507	D 2 X	.0250	.964
19	.0359	.506	D 3 X	.0281	1.102
20	.0320	.450	D 4 X	.0313	1.231
21	.0285	.401			
22	.0253	.357			
23	.0226	.318	NOTE: The above is thickness of		
24	.0201	.283	black sheet iron before		
25	.0179	.252	tinning.		

METAL GAUGE AND RIVET SIZES

GAUGE OF METAL USED FOR ROUND PIPES

OR RECTANGULAR DUCTS

Size in Inches	1 to 12	13 to 30	31 to 42	43 to 60	61 and up
Gauge	26	24	22	20	18

FLATHEAD RIVETS

Size Weight per 1000 Rivets Oz. and Lb.	Diameter	Length
4 oz.	.070	$1/8$
6	.080	$9/64$
8	.090	$5/32$
10	.094	$11/64$
12	.101	$3/16$
14	.109	$3/16$
1 lb.	.115	$13/64$
$1\frac{1}{4}$	.120	$7/32$
$1\frac{1}{2}$	.125	$15/64$
$1\frac{3}{4}$	.133	$1/4$
2	.140	$17/64$
$2\frac{1}{2}$	.147	$9/32$
3	.160	$5/16$
$3\frac{1}{2}$	.163	$21/64$
4	.173	$11/32$
5	.185	$3/8$
6	.200	$25/64$
7	.215	$13/32$
8	.225	$7/16$
9	.230	$29/64$
10	.233	$15/32$
12	.253	$1/2$
14	.275	$33/64$
16	.293	$17/32$

MEASURES

Linear Measure

12 inches = 1 foot
3 feet   = 1 yard

The word inch or inches may be indicated by the abbreviation *in.*, or by the symbol (″). A measurement of 3 inches is expressed as 3 in. or 3″. The abbreviation for foot, or its plural, feet, is *ft.*; the symbol is (′). The measurement of 4 feet would be expressed as 4 ft. or 4′.

Board Measures

A board foot (bd. ft.) is equal to a piece of lumber one foot long, one foot wide, and one inch thick: 12″ × 12″ × 1″.

Square Measure

A square foot is equal to the length times the width.

(12″ × 12″) 144 square inches (sq. in.) = 1 square foot (sq. ft.)
(3′ × 3′)   9 square feet   = 1 square yard (sq. yd.)
          100 square feet   = 1 square

Cubic Measure

Cubic measure deals with three dimensions: length, width, and thickness. The abbreviation for cubic inches is (cu. in.). In square measures we find that a square foot is equal to length × width (12″ × 12″ = 144 sq. in.). In cubic inches we must first obtain the square inches. The cubic inches are obtained by multiplying the product of the base or one side by the height or thickness, such as length times width times the height. The cubic inches in a 12-inch cube are equal to 12 × 12 × 12 or 1728 cubic inches (or 12 × 12 = 144 sq. in. × 12 = 1728 cu. in.).

1728 cubic inches (cu. in.) = 1 cubic foot (cu. ft.)
27 cubic feet   = 1 cubic yard (cu. yd.)

Avoirdupois or Commercial Weight

16 ounces (oz.) = 1 pound (lb.)
100 pounds = 1 hundredweight (cwt.)
20 hundredweight = 1 long ton (T) = 2240 pounds

Liquid Measure

16 fluid ounces = 1 pint
2 pints   = 1 quart
4 quarts   = 1 gallon
3½ gallons = 1 barrel

A gallon of water at 62 deg. F. weighs 8.3356 pounds.
The U.S. gallon contains 231 cubic inches.

Dry Measure

2 pints or 57.75 cu. in. = 1 quart
4 quarts or 231 cu. in. = 1 gallon
2 gallons or 8 quarts = 1 peck
4 pecks or 2150.42 cu. in. = 1 bushel
1 gallon = 231 cu. in. or 1.34 cu. ft.
7.48 gallons = 1 cu. ft.
1 liquid quart = $57\frac{3}{4}$ cu. in.
1 gallon water = $8\frac{1}{3}$ lb.
1 gallon gasoline = 5.84 lb.
1 gallon linseed oil = 7.84 lb.
1 cu. ft. of water weighs $62\frac{1}{2}$ lb.
1 cu. ft. of ice weighs 57.25 lb.

Angles are measured in degrees, minutes, and seconds.

1 degree = 60 minutes
1 minute = 60 seconds
1 circle = 360 degrees

Symbols are commonly used as follows:

Degrees = °
Minutes = ′
Seconds = ″

For example, 35 degrees, 23 minutes, and 41 seconds is written 35° 23′ 41″.

DECIMALS TO FRACTIONS

In calculating sheet-metal work, the results often are in decimals. When laying out a job with decimals involved, they must be changed to fractions so they can be read on a rule. This may be done mentally or mathematically.

To determine the fractional equivalents, the results often need to be carried only to the nearest $\frac{1}{16}$ of an inch. If, therefore, the results obtained in an answer have decimals, reduce them to the nearest $\frac{1}{16}$ of an inch.

To do this, multiply the decimal portion of the answer by 16. Thus, if the answer is 4.82, multiply the .82 by 16. .82 × 16 = 13.12 sixteenths, say $\frac{13}{16}$ in. The answer, then, is given the value of $4\frac{13}{16}$.

To change a decimal to 8ths, multiply the decimal by 8. To change a decimal to 32nds, multiply the decimal by 32.

These conversions can be made more readily if the following table is committed to memory:

.875 in. = $\frac{7}{8}$ in.   .75 in. = $\frac{3}{4}$ in.   .5   in. = $\frac{1}{2}$ in.
.250 in. = $\frac{1}{4}$ in.   .125 in. = $\frac{1}{8}$ in.   .0625 in. = $\frac{1}{16}$ in.
.03125 in. = $\frac{1}{32}$ in.

METRIC CONVERSION FACTORS

Unit	Inches to Millimeters	Millimeters to Inches	Pounds to Kilograms	Kilograms to Pounds
1	25.4001	039371	0.45359	2.20462
2	50.8001	078742	0.90719	4.40924
3	76.2002	118112	1.36078	6.61386
4	101.6002	157483	1.81437	8.81849
5	127.0003	196854	2.26796	11.02311
6	152.4003	236225	2.72156	13.22773
7	177.8004	275596	3.17515	15.43235
8	203.2004	314966	3.62874	17.63697
9	228.6005	354337	4.08233	19.84159
10	254.0006	393708	4.35592	22.04622

1 gram = 15,432 grains
1 meter = 39.371 in. or 3.28083 ft.
1 millimeter = 0.03937 in., or $\frac{1}{25}$ in. approx.
1 metric ton or 1000 kilograms = 2204.6 lb. or .9842 ton of 2240 lb.
1.016 metric ton or 1016 kilograms = 1 ton of 2240 lb.
1 kilogram per sq. centimeter = 14.2234 lb. per sq. in.
1 kilogram per sq. millimeter = 1422.32 lb. per sq. in.
1000 lb. per sq. in. = 0.70308 kilo per sq. mi. or 70.308 kilo. per sq. cm.

MEASUREMENTS

Areas

Parallelogram	= base × altitude.
Triangle	= half base × altitude.
Trapezoid	= half the sum of the two parallel sides × the perpendicular distance between them.
Regular polygon	= half the perimeter × the perpendicular distance from the center to any one side.
Circle	= square of the diameter × .7854.
Sector of circle	= number of degrees in arc × square of radius × 0.008727.
Segment of circle	= area of sector with same arc − area of triangle formed by radii of the arc and chord of the segment.
Octagon	= square of diameter of inscribed circle × .828.
Hexagon	= square of diameter of inscribed circle × .866.
Sphere	= area of its great circle × 4; or square of diameter × 3.14159.

Volumes

Prism	= area of base × altitude.
Wedge	= length of edge + twice length of base × one-sixth of the product of the height of the wedge and the breadth of its base.
Cylinder	= area of base × altitude.
Cone	= area of base × one third of altitude.
Sphere	= cube of diameter × 0.5236.

Miscellaneous

Diameter of circle	= circumference × .31831.
Circumference of circle	= diameter × 3.1416.

DECIMAL EQUIVALENTS OF ONE INCH

$\frac{1}{64} = .015625$	$\frac{11}{32} = .34375$	$\frac{11}{16} = .6875$
$\frac{1}{32} = .03125$	$\frac{23}{64} = .359375$	$\frac{45}{64} = .703125$
$\frac{3}{64} = .046875$	$\frac{3}{8} = .375$	$\frac{23}{32} = .71875$
$\frac{1}{16} = .0625$	$\frac{25}{64} = .390625$	$\frac{47}{64} = .734375$
$\frac{5}{64} = .078125$	$\frac{13}{32} = .40625$	$\frac{3}{4} = .75$
$\frac{3}{32} = .09375$	$\frac{27}{64} = .421875$	$\frac{49}{64} = .765625$
$\frac{7}{64} = .109375$	$\frac{7}{16} = .4375$	$\frac{25}{32} = .78125$
$\frac{1}{8} = .125$	$\frac{29}{64} = .453125$	$\frac{51}{64} = .796875$
$\frac{9}{64} = .140265$	$\frac{15}{32} = .46875$	$\frac{13}{16} = .8125$
$\frac{5}{32} = .15625$	$\frac{31}{64} = .484375$	$\frac{53}{64} = .828125$
$\frac{11}{64} = .171875$	$\frac{1}{2} = .5$	$\frac{27}{32} = .84375$
$\frac{3}{16} = .1875$	$\frac{33}{64} = .515625$	$\frac{55}{64} = .859375$
$\frac{13}{64} = .203125$	$\frac{17}{32} = .53125$	$\frac{7}{8} = .875$
$\frac{7}{32} = .21875$	$\frac{35}{64} = .546875$	$\frac{57}{64} = .890625$
$\frac{15}{64} = .234375$	$\frac{9}{16} = .5625$	$\frac{29}{32} = .90625$
$\frac{1}{4} = .25$	$\frac{37}{64} = .578125$	$\frac{59}{64} = .921875$
$\frac{17}{64} = .265625$	$\frac{19}{32} = .59375$	$\frac{15}{16} = .9375$
$\frac{9}{32} = .28125$	$\frac{39}{64} = .609375$	$\frac{61}{64} = .953125$
$\frac{19}{64} = .296875$	$\frac{5}{8} = .625$	$\frac{31}{32} = .96875$
$\frac{5}{16} = .3125$	$\frac{41}{64} = .640625$	$\frac{63}{64} = .984375$
$\frac{21}{64} = .328125$	$\frac{21}{32} = .65625$	$1 = 1.$
	$\frac{43}{64} = .671875$	

CIRCUMFERENCES AND AREAS OF CIRCLES

	Of One Inch				*Of Inches or Feet*	
Fract.	*Dec.*	*Circ.*	*Area*	*Dia*	*Circ.*	*Area*
1/64	.015625	.04909	.00019	1	3.1416	.7854
1/32	.03125	.09818	.00077	2	6.2832	3.1416
3/64	.046875	.14726	.00173	3	9.4248	7.0686
1/16	.0625	.19635	.00307	4	12.5664	12.5664
5/64	.078125	.24545	.00479	5	15.708	19.635
3/32	.09375	.29452	.00690	6	18.850	28.274
7/64	.109375	.34363	.00939	7	21.991	38.485
1/8	.125	.39270	.01227	8	25.133	50.265
9/64	.140625	.44181	.01553	9	28.274	63.617
5/32	.15625	.49087	.01917	10	31.416	78.540
11/64	.171875	.53999	.02320	11	34.558	95.033
3/16	.1875	.58905	.02761	12	37.699	113.10
13/64	.203125	.63817	.03241	13	40.841	132.73
7/32	.21875	.68722	.03758	14	43.982	153.94
15/64	.234375	.73635	.04314	15	47.124	176.71
1/4	.25	.78540	.04909	16	50.265	201.06
17/64	.265625	.83453	.05542	17	53.407	226.98
9/32	.28125	.88357	.06213	18	56.549	254.47
19/64	.296875	.93271	.06922	19	59.690	283.53
5/16	.3125	.98175	.07670	20	62.832	314.16
21/64	.328125	1.0309	.08456	21	65.973	346.36
11/32	.34375	1.0799	.09281	22	69.115	380.13
23/64	.359375	1.1291	.10144	23	72.257	415.48
3/8	.375	1.1781	.11045	24	75.398	452.39
25/64	.390625	1.2273	.11984	25	78.540	490.87
13/32	.40625	1.2763	.12962	26	81.681	530.93
27/64	.421875	1.3254	.13979	27	84.823	572.56
7/16	.4375	1.3744	.15033	28	87.965	615.75
29/64	.453125	1.4236	.16126	29	91.106	660.52
15/32	.46875	1.4726	.17257	30	94.248	706.86
31/64	.484375	1.5218	.18427	31	97.389	754.77
1/2	.5	1.5708	.19635	32´	100.53	804.25
33/64	.515625	1.6199	.20880	33	103.67	855.30
17/32	.53125	1.6690	.22166	34	106.81	907.92
35/64	.546875	1.7181	.23489	35	109.96	962.11
9/16	.5625	1.7671	.24850	36	113.10	1017.88
37/64	.578125	1.8163	.26248	37	116.24	1075.21
19/32	.59375	1.8653	.27688	38	119.38	1134.11
39/64	.609375	1.9145	.29164	39	122.52	1194.59
5/8	.625	1.9635	.30680	40	125.66	1256.64
41/64	.640625	2.0127	.32232	41	128.81	1320.25

Of One Inch				Of Inches or Feet		
Fract.	Dec.	Circ.	Area	Dia.	Circ.	Area
$^{21}/_{32}$	.65625	2.0617	.33824	42	131.95	1385.44
$^{43}/_{64}$	.671875	2.1108	.35453	43	135.09	1452.20
$^{11}/_{16}$	.6875	2.1598	.37122	44	138.23	1520.53
$^{45}/_{64}$	.703125	2.2090	.38828	45	141.37	1590.43
$^{23}/_{32}$	.71875	2.2580	.40574	46	144.51	1661.90
$^{47}/_{64}$	.734375	2.3072	.42356	47	147.65	1734.94
$^{3}/_{4}$	.75	2.3562	.44179	48	150.80	1809.56
$^{49}/_{64}$	.765625	2.4054	.45253	49	153.94	1885.74
$^{25}/_{32}$	.78125	2.4544	.47937	50	157.08	1963.50
$^{51}/_{64}$	.796875	2.5036	.49872	51	160.22	2042.82
$^{13}/_{16}$	.8125	2.5525	.51849	52	163.36	2123.72
$^{53}/_{64}$	.828125	2.6017	.53862	53	166.50	2206.18
$^{27}/_{32}$	.84375	2.6507	.55914	54	169.65	2290.22
$^{55}/_{64}$	.859375	2.6999	.58003	55	172.79	2375.83
$^{7}/_{8}$	.875	2.7489	.60132	56	175.93	2463.01
$^{57}/_{64}$	.890625	2.7981	.62298	57	179.07	2551.76
$^{29}/_{32}$	.90625	2.8471	.64504	58	182.21	2642.08
$^{59}/_{64}$	.921875	2.8963	.66746	59	185.35	2733.97
$^{15}/_{16}$	.9375	2.9452	.69029	60	188.50	2827.43
$^{61}/_{64}$	.953125	2.9945	.71349	61	191.64	2922.47
$^{31}/_{32}$	.96875	3.0434	.73708	62	194.78	3019.07
$^{63}/_{64}$	.984375	3.0928	.76097	63	197.92	3117.25

Of Inches or Feet			Of Inches or Feet		
Dia.	Circ.	Area	Dia.	Circ.	Area
64	201.06	3216.99	96	301.59	7238.23
65	204.20	3318.31	97	304.73	7389.81
66	207.34	3421.19	98	307.88	7542.96
67	210.49	3525.65	99	311.02	7697.69
68	213.63	3631.68	100	314.16	7853.98
69	216.77	3739.28	101	317.30	8011.85
70	219.91	3848.45	102	320.44	8171.28
71	223.05	3959.19	103	323.58	8332.29
72	226.19	4071.50	104	326.73	8494.87
73	229.34	4185.39	105	329.87	8659.01
74	232.48	4300.84	106	333.01	8824.73
75	235.62	4417.86	107	336.15	8992.02
76	238.76	4536.46	108	339.29	9160.88
77	241.90	4656.63	109	342.43	9331.32
78	245.04	4778.36	110	345.58	9503.32
79	248.19	4901.67	111	348.72	9676.89

CIRCUMFERENCES AND AREAS OF CIRCLES (CONT.)

	Of Inches or Feet			Of Inches or Feet	
Dia.	Circ.	Area	Dia.	Circ.	Area
80	251.33	5026.55	112	351.86	9852.03
81	254.47	5153.00	113	355.00	10028.75
82	257.61	5281.02	114	358.14	10207.03
83	260.75	5410.61	115	361.28	10386.89
84	263.89	5541.77	116	364.42	10568.32
85	267.04	5674.50	117	367.57	10751.32
86	270.18	5808.80	118	370.71	10935.88
87	273.32	5944.68	119	373.85	11122.02
88	276.46	6082.12	120	376.99	11309.73
89	279.60	6221.14	121	380.13	11499.01
90	282.74	6361.73	122	383.27	11689.87
91	285.88	6503.88	123	386.42	11882.29
92	289.03	6647.61	124	389.56	12076.28
93	292.17	6792.91	125	392.70	12271.85
94	295.31	6939.78	126	395.84	12468.98
95	298.45	7088.22			